An Eye for An Eye

An Eye for An Eye

The Immorality of Punishing by Death

2nd Edition

STEPHEN NATHANSON

ROWMAN & LITTLEFIELD PUBLISHERS, INC.
Lanham • Boulder • New York • Oxford

To Ursula Bentele and Bill Bowers—
committed scholars, cherished friends.

ROWMAN & LITTLEFIELD PUBLISHERS, INC.

Published in the United States of America
by Rowman & Littlefield Publishers, Inc.
4720 Boston Way, Lanham, Maryland 20706
www.rowmanlittlefield.com

12 Hid's Copse Road
Cumnor Hill, Oxford OX2 9JJ, England

British Library Cataloguing in Publication Information Available

Library of Congress Cataloging-in-Publication Data

Nathanson, Stephen, 1943–
    An eye for an eye : the immorality of punishing by death / Stephen Nathanson.
    — 2nd ed.
      p. cm.
    Includes bibliographical references (p.) and index.
    ISBN 0-7425-1325-4 (alk. paper) — ISBN 0-7425-1326-2 (pbk. : alk. paper)
    1. Capital punishment. I. Title.

  HV8694 .N37 2001
  364.66—dc21

                            2001049208

Printed in the United States of America

♾™ The paper used in this publication meets the minimum requirements of American
National Standard for Information Sciences—Permanence of Paper for Printed Library
Materials, ANSI/NISO Z39.48-1992.

Contents

Foreword

I, LIKE THE AUTHOR OF THIS EXCELLENT BOOK, am opposed to the death penalty. I believe with Camus and Mr. Nathanson that we should take the "great civilizing step" of abolishing it. To my great regret, the Supreme Court has decided otherwise.

The Eighth Amendment to the Constitution prohibits cruel and unusual punishment. That the death penalty is cruel, no one can deny. That it is unusual is established by the fact that juries are increasingly reluctant to impose it. And most civilized nations, e.g., Great Britain and France, have abolished it.

My objection has been expressed, in main part, on legal grounds, although it is also based on moral considerations.

It is highly unlikely that the present Supreme Court will change its collective mind. And it is equally unlikely that state legislatures, in light of recent polls, will change theirs. Mr. Nathanson may be more optimistic, and he may prove to be right. Time works changes and we may, in time, become more civilized.

Mr. Nathanson notes that many people of good will support capital punishment, and he sets out to provide them with the factual information and the moral reasoning that shows capital punishment to be unnecessary to our safety, unjustly discriminatory in its application, and in violation of widely held moral principles and ideals. By carefully considering many of the arguments expressed by supporters and opponents of capital punishment, Mr. Nathanson makes clear which considerations remain intact after being subjected to careful scrutiny.

Finally, Mr. Nathanson contends that we must acquaint people with the fact that the execution of innocent people is a real possibility. We do not have a foolproof system, and recent studies show that some innocent people have been executed and many have come close to execution. In addition to acquainting the general public with the facts about capital punishment, opponents of the death penalty should, despite present rebuffs, as a matter of conscience, appeal to people's moral sensitivities. This is the primary task Stephen Nathanson has set for himself in *An Eye for an Eye?*

Arthur J. Goldberg, former Associate Justice, the Supreme Court of the United States

Preface to the Second Edition

THE DEATH PENALTY QUESTION has not gone away in the years since 1987, when the first edition of this book was published, and the need for more knowledge and better thinking about it is as great as ever. This book first appeared during a period of extremely strong support for the death penalty. While support remains strong today, indications are that the current time may be more receptive to arguments against the death penalty.

After years of actual experience with executions, there is a greater awareness of defects in the death penalty system. We have all heard about people being released from death row after DNA evidence proved their innocence. We have heard about incompetent defense lawyers representing people facing the possibility of a death sentence. We have become more aware of the impact of race and economic class on death sentences. And, in a period of lower crime rates, we may be collectively less fearful and more able to look at the situation more deliberatively.

Even while an apparently clear case like that of Timothy McVeigh seems to vindicate capital punishment, this same case raised many doubts and exposed public ambivalence about executions. McVeigh's bombing of the federal building in Oklahoma City certainly counts as a horrific murder—168 dead and many injured. Yet his execution by lethal injection seems unlikely to have provided solace, satisfaction, or "closure" to victims' families. The discussion of a televised execution excited both interest and revulsion. The opposition to McVeigh's execution by some of the victims' families undermines the old retort: "Well, if your loved one were killed, you'd feel differently about this." The failure of the FBI to provide full documentation to lawyers in the case shows that even in the highest profile cases, errors and procedural violations are made. The evidence made no difference in

McVeigh's case—he was executed anyway—but surely there are other cases in which similar lapses were never exposed and could have meant the difference between life and death or even guilt and innocence.

Another change is the solidifying international opposition to the death penalty. The United States now stands virtually alone among developed countries in its retention of punishing by death. Others look at us as anomalies and wonder why we continue a practice that they have rejected.

While the death penalty persists in the United States, the reasons against it persist as well. Because the arguments I developed in the book have retained their relevance and timeliness, I have left them in their original form in this new edition. The revisions I have made take the form of a postscript, whose contents supplement but do not supplant the discussions that appeared in the original edition and that continue to make up the bulk of this version.

I take advantage of this opportunity both to put the death penalty debate in perspective and to add some new arguments. The new material discusses why the death penalty debate seems to elude resolution and whether this shows it to be a "gut issue" that cannot be resolved by rational means. I offer some evidence that beliefs about the death penalty are—in spite of appearances to the contrary—at least partly a function of reasoning and evidence. At the same time, I try to show why it is difficult to produce knockdown arguments for one side or another. Finally, I make a new attempt to state the case against capital punishment in a reasoned but forceful way. I hope that these new arguments will be persuasive and compelling—even with death penalty supporters.

Like its predecessor, this new edition is an expression of my own moral and intellectual ideals. It flows from a commitment to the value of rational, respectful debate and a belief in the need for constraints on human violence. I hope that the book can contribute in some small way toward strengthening the place of these ideals in our lives.

Preface

THIS BOOK IS THE PRODUCT of my attempt to resolve the issue of whether the death penalty is a morally legitimate means of punishment. In it, I consider the most important arguments for and against using death as a punishment, and I conclude that the death penalty is not morally acceptable.

While my conclusion places me among those who favor abolition of the death penalty and while I do argue forcefully against its use, I have not written a diatribe or polemic. As a citizen and a human being, I am motivated to speak out against the evil of executions, but as a philosopher, I want to understand, explain, and assess the reasons and arguments offered on both sides of the debate.

Thus, while I am no friend of the death penalty, I write with no animus toward its supporters, and I have tried to give their arguments a fair hearing. There are, of course, political leaders and others who advocate capital punishment as part of a calculated attempt to gain or maintain power, but most people who favor the death penalty are motivated by natural reactions of fear and indignation, as well as laudatory moral desires to protect the innocent and to see justice done. So, I shall not assume that support for the death penalty flows from callousness or insensitivity, and I shall try to take the concerns of death penalty supporters seriously.

To many people, the very idea of a rational assessment of arguments about the death penalty will seem absurd and doomed to failure. The death penalty controversy has become the epitome of the unresolvable issue, the question which people answer on the basis of gut reactions rather than logical arguments. From this perspective, it is hopeless to adopt a rational approach to the issue. Confronting the significant public support which now exists for capital punishment with rational arguments might be compared to trying to move a mountain by saying "please."

While I agree that it would be foolish to expect that this book by itself will transform public attitudes toward executions, I disagree that the death penalty issue is a matter to be decided by the gut rather than the head. Part of my goal in writing the book is to show that we can reason our way through difficult moral questions if we are willing to use our heads for serious thought. All too frequently, calling something a "gut issue" is no more than a cloak for hiding our own unwillingness to expose our views to debate or to think hard about them.

So, while not being foolishly optimistic about the power of reason to alter widespread social attitudes, I would like to show that reason is not impotent, and I would urge that we be wary of surrendering too much to the realm of the gut. In any case, one way of showing something to be other than a gut issue is to discuss it rationally, and that is what I have attempted to do. If my arguments are weak or inconclusive, then they can be improved by death penalty opponents or refuted by death penalty supporters.

We need not have reasons for everything that we do, but taking people's lives is a very serious matter. If we choose to impose death as a punishment, we need strong reasons to justify our choice. To proceed without reason in this case shows indifference not only to rationalist values but also, and more importantly, to human life itself.

In spite of widespread doubts about the possibility of reasoning about the morality of executions, people readily cite many reasons for their views on this issue. My procedure in the book is simply to formulate the arguments offered on both sides and to see whether they provide good reasons for the position they are meant to defend. In order to carry out this plan, we will need to consider the following questions:

1. Is the death penalty immoral because it is the same as murder?
2. Are executions justified as a way of showing respect for the lives of murder victims?
3. Are executions justified because they deter potential murderers and thus save innocent lives?
4. Should we adopt the death penalty because it is cheaper to execute murderers than to imprison them?
5. Is the death penalty immoral because discrimination and

other arbitrary factors influence decisions about which murderers are actually executed?

6. Is the death penalty justified because murderers deserve to die?
7. Is the death penalty a "cruel and unusual" punishment?
8. Does the desire for vengeance against murderers justify executions?
9. Does the morality or immorality of the death penalty depend entirely on whether it deters murders better than other punishments?
10. What symbolic messages about our society and its values are conveyed by the practice of executing murderers?
11. What symbolic messages about our society and its values are conveyed by deciding not to execute murderers?

These are the questions that need to be answered in order to arrive at a considered judgment about the morality of the death penalty. In the chapters that follow, I will address all of these questions and try to show that the best answers to them lead to a moral condemnation of the practice of punishing by death.

During the time this book has been in production, the Supreme Court has issued two decisions—*McCleskey v. Kemp* and *Tison v. Arizona*—that affirm the constitutional legitimacy of the death penalty within our legal system. For opponents of the death penalty, these decisions have been a serious setback. This is not to say that this constitutional issue has been finally laid to rest. Both decisions were upheld by bare five to four majorities, and the majority view is open to criticism.

Nonetheless, even if the Court's current constitutional judgment is sustained in the future, that does not directly affect the issues as I have approached them here. Only nine people sit on the Supreme Court, and their task is to interpret the Constitution. When the rest of us confront the issue of the death penalty, it is as individual citizens who want a morally just society. Our reflections and judgments are about the *morality* (and not the constitutionality) of the death penalty. While judicial decisions are critically important within the legal system, they are not decisive in the realm of morality. Whether the arguments of this book are valid and, more important, whether the death penalty is morally legitimate are issues that call for individual judgments from all of us.

Acknowledgments

THIS BOOK would not have been written without the interest and encouragement of a number of people, and many improvements in the book resulted from their criticisms and responses to it. It is a pleasure to express my deep appreciation to Hugo Bedau, Ursula Bentele, William Bowers, Nelson Lande, Peter Smith, and John Troyer for sharing their knowledge and their reactions to my thinking.

I am indebted to Northeastern University for the period of sabbatical leave in which I was able to collect my thoughts and form them into this book. Thanks, too, to Michael Lipton for very helpful advice and assistance with word processing and to the many friends, colleagues, and students with whom I have discussed the death penalty over the years.

As always, Linda, Michael, and Sarah have been my most prized sources of inspiration and support.

Portions of chapters 4 and 5 appeared previously in my paper "Does It Matter if the Death Penalty Is Arbitrarily Administered?" *Philosophy and Public Affairs* 14, no. 2 (Spring 1985). Reprinted with permission of Princeton University Press.

Grateful acknowledgment is also made to Ernest van den Haag for permission to quote from "The Collapse of the Case Against Capital Punishment," *National Review,* March 31, 1978.

In preparing this new edition, I would like to thank especially Ursula Bentele and Bill Bowers for being inspiring models of commitment to a cause over the long haul, for help in keeping me educated on the subject of the death penalty, for insightful criticisms, and for encouraging responses to my work. As an expression of my appreciation and admiration, I dedicate this book to Bill and Ursula. Thanks, too, to Jon Sisk and Eve DeVaro of Rowman & Littlefield for their interest in bringing out a second edition of this work. Finally, I thank my wife, Linda, for suggestions about the postscript and for her loving support in all that I do.

|1|

Respect For Life

THE DEATH PENALTY has been imposed throughout history for many crimes, ranging from blasphemy and treason to picking pockets and piracy. For the most part, contemporary debate centers on the death penalty as a punishment for murder, and all of the arguments I will consider have this focus.

One of the most paradoxical features of the death penalty debate is that people on both sides see themselves as defenders of the value of life and see their opponents as failing to take the value of life seriously enough. From the point of view of death penalty opponents, those who support executions show a lack of appropriate respect for life by favoring needless killings. The problem is magnified if the number of people to be executed is large, for the result appears to be a legal massacre. From the standpoint of death penalty supporters, however, people who oppose the death penalty are insufficiently respectful of the lives of murder victims. For death penalty supporters, it is appalling that the punishment for so dreadful a crime as murder should be anything less than death itself.

So both sides seek to show their respect for life, but they differ about the appropriate way of doing so. One side thinks that respect for life forbids the use of the death penalty, while the other believes that respect for life requires it. For many people on both sides of the debate, the issue is simple and clear-cut, and they find it difficult to understand how anyone could see things differently.

As a first step toward understanding and resolving the issue, we need to see that the problem is not as simple as many think. To do this, I shall try to formulate the arguments based on respect for life that underlie and support each position. When the reasons for both views have been exposed, we will be in a better position to assess them.

The Death Penalty as Legal Murder

To opponents of the death penalty, it is absurd to engage in deliberate killing and to call this a means of expressing one's respect for life. The primary way to show respect for life is to avoid killing. One does not commit murder in order to show that murder is wrong. This makes no more sense than defacing a beautiful building to show that defacing beautiful buildings is wrong. The death penalty, they argue, is the same act as murder, and both are wrong because both are acts of killing.

One way to capture the reasoning involved in this view is through the following argument:

1. Murder is wrong.
2. The death penalty is a form of murder.
3. Therefore, the death penalty is wrong.

In viewing this argument, I take it that neither side would deny that the first premise, "murder is wrong," is true. (By "wrong," I mean *morally* wrong, as I shall throughout this discussion.) This is not because it is impossible to dispute this. Various moral skeptics or relativists might reject this idea, claiming that we cannot know the truth of any moral belief. Certain kinds of racists or other elitists might believe that killing "inferior" persons is permitted or even required by morality. Such views raise issues which are worth discussing, but I shall not discuss them here. Every respectable party to the death penalty debate agrees that murder is wrong, and we are simply not concerned here with those who deny the immorality of murder or have no respect for the value of life.

The second thing to note about the argument (that the death penalty is wrong because it is a form of murder) is that it is logically valid. That is, *if* the statements numbered 1 and 2 are both true, then the conclusion is true. One could not agree that murder is wrong and that the death penalty is a form of murder, and then reject the conclusion that the death penalty is wrong.

Since the argument is logically valid and the first premise is true, the only way to avoid accepting the conclusion is by rejecting the second premise, "The death penalty is a form of murder." This, of course, is just what death penalty supporters would do. They do not see executions as a form of murder.

For many, however, an execution is a form of murder because it is the very same act as murder. When one person murders another, he deliberately takes some action (such as firing a gun, administering a poison, producing a powerful electric shock), intending that this will result in the death of another person. When an execution occurs, the very same thing takes place. A process is deliberately initiated with the intention that it result in the death of a person. So, it is argued, murder and execution are identical actions, and if one is morally wrong, so is the other.

While this argument is not totally without merit, it relies on too simple a view of what makes two actions "the same." It is possible for two actions to share many features, indeed to be physically identical, and yet for them to be quite different acts. Consider the following case: A woman enters a bank, gives the teller a slip of paper, receives a sum of money from him, and leaves. She then goes to another bank and does the very same thing. She appears to have done the same act twice. Nonetheless, the first act was a legal transaction (withdrawing money from her account), while the second was a bank robbery. That the two acts are identical in many respects does not mean that they are the very same act. The crucial difference between the legal transaction and the robbery concerns whether she was legally authorized to withdraw the money. That is what distinguishes an ordinary person's visit to the bank from that of a bank robber.

For death penalty supporters, the difference between legal executions and murder is like the difference between legal withdrawals from one's own bank account and bank robbery. They may look the same, but they are essentially different. Many examples can be offered to show that very similar acts are described and classified differently because of the context in which they occur. One person walks across a field and does nothing wrong because he owns it. A second person walks across the same field in the same way and is guilty of trespassing on private property. Two authors submit manuscripts to a publisher. One of them is acting quite properly, while the other is engaging in plagiarism, having copied the ideas of the first.

What all these examples show is that whether two acts are the same is not a simple matter. It does not follow from the physical similarities between murder and execution that they are the same. Here, as in other cases, the legal status of the action may make all the difference in the world. By *assuming* that executions are murders, death penalty opponents are begging the question, for they are assuming that the legal status of a killing makes no difference to whether it is murder.

The real value of "the death penalty is murder" argument is that it forces death penalty advocates to specify how murder and executions differ. They may, of course, simply point to the fact that executions (where properly authorized by law) are in fact legal, but this by itself will not show that executions are morally legitimate. Legality and morality are quite different. Many examples could be given to show that the legality of an action does not establish its moral rightness, but the point is made starkly clear in some comments by Richard Rubenstein about the Nazi death camps. "The Jews were executed in accordance with German law," he writes, and so "the Nazis committed no crime at Auschwitz. . . ."[1]

While Rubenstein is himself skeptical about appeals to a "higher moral law," most of us would not hesitate to say that the deeds done at Auschwitz were moral crimes, even if they were perfectly legal. Similarly, when murderers are executed in accord with due process of law, the fact that nothing illegal has been done provides no guarantee that the execution was morally right.

Death penalty opponents are correct, then, in asserting that we cannot equate morality and legality. Nonetheless, this by itself does not advance their case. It is not enough for them to to show that legal acts *may* be immoral. They need to show that legal executions actually are immoral, and the argument we have considered does not establish this. It fails because it assumes what it ought to prove—that executions and murders are morally on a par. Let us turn to a related argument which does not have this drawback.

The Wrongness of Killing

Death penalty opponents might contend that while the morality of walking on someone's property or of taking money from the bank is affected by whether the property and the money belong to a person, mere legality does not affect the morality of killing someone. Deliberate killing simply is murder, whether or not it is legally sanctioned, because all deliberate killing is morally wrong.

Here, again, it will be useful to make the argument completely explicit so that we can gauge its worth. We can express it in the following form:

1. The death penalty is a form of deliberate killing.
2. All deliberate killing is wrong.
3. Therefore, the death penalty is wrong.

This argument is an advance over the first because it does not simply label the death penalty murder. Instead, it focuses on the crucial element that makes executions wrong, the fact that they are deliberate acts of killing. Because all such acts are wrong, the death penalty is wrong.

Like its predecessor, this argument is logically valid. Its conclusion really does follow from its premises. Likewise, it contains one premise which is obviously true. No one would dispute the claim that the death penalty is a form of deliberate killing. So, the strength of the argument depends on the second premise, the statement that all deliberate killing is wrong.

The idea that all deliberate killing is wrong is not without force. Not killing would appear to be the best way to show respect for life. In addition, the principle echoes the biblical command "Thou shalt not kill." We know, too, how much evil has been done by those who have thought that they could legitimately take life, and it is appealing to dissociate oneself entirely from the callous presumptuousness with which so many have acted.

Nonetheless, in spite of the appeal of this principle, it conflicts with moral common sense, and there are good reasons for rejecting it. Taken literally, the view that *all* deliberate killing is wrong would forbid many actions which people find acceptable. Most people believe that it is permissible to kill nonhuman animals for food. Even vegetarians, who condemn this practice (especially if it is unnecessary for human survival), would presumably not object to killing insects, especially if they are carriers of disease.

Moreover, even if we understand this principle to forbid only the taking of human life, almost all of us believe that there are cases in which killing human beings is morally permissible. The clearest cases are those in which killing an attacker is the only way to defend one's own life or the life of another person. When someone kills in self-defense or in defense of a loved one and when there is no alternative way of saving oneself or another from death by attack, we do not condemn this person or his action. We think that the action is not simply excusable but that it is justifiable.

If we understand the principle that all deliberate killing is wrong strictly and literally, it forbids actions which most of us believe are morally right. If actions can violate the principle and still be morally right, then we should reject the principle that all deliberate killing is wrong. In rejecting this principle, of course, we are not saying that killing is always right and that one can take the life of others whenever one feels like it or for any reasons whatsoever. That would be absurd. Rather, we are saying that there are *justifiable exceptions* to the principle which forbids killing. Instead of thinking of the correct moral rule as finding expression in the words "All killing is wrong," we would want to express it by saying: "In general, killing is wrong," or "Killing is wrong, except in the following cases:. . . ."

Once we reject the principle that all deliberate killing is wrong, then the second argument against the death penalty collapses. For if we grant that there are some justifiable exceptions to the moral principle forbidding killing, then it may be that the execution of murderers by the state is one of these exceptions.

Absolute Pacifism

In rejecting the idea that all deliberate killing of human beings is wrong, I have offered examples of killing in self-defense or defense of others (when this is the only way to save their lives) as cases of morally justified killings. By and large, this is not a controversial matter. Most people would accept it. Nonetheless, it is not universally accepted and would be rejected by the absolute pacifist, the person for whom acts of killing (and perhaps all violent acts) are so terrible that they may not be performed even to defend one's life or the life of another. A person whose opposition to the death penalty is rooted in a general pacifist position would be unmoved by what I have written so far.

We could simply ignore the pacifist view. Most people who cite the "killing is wrong" principle when arguing about the death penalty are not in fact pacifists. By considering cases like killing in self-defense, they would come to see that they cannot base their opposition to the death penalty on a total rejection of killing. Moreover, the pacifist position is so much of a minority view that if it turned out that pacifism provided the only basis for opposition to the death penalty, that would simply increase the problem of showing that the death penalty is morally wrong.

Nonetheless, pacifists, more than most of us, have striven to warn us against the casual taking of life and have worked to search for alternatives to the methods of violence to which most societies have become accustomed. Their rejection of all killing, then, deserves at least an answer from those of us who accept some deliberate killings as morally justified.

The answer to absolute pacifism has two parts. The first is based on the idea that people have a right to life. Although there are many difficult questions about rights, one generally accepted feature of them is that a person with a right to something is morally permitted to take steps to prevent others from violating that right. If I have a right to privacy on my property, then I can legitimately build a fence, order someone to leave, or call on the police to remove the intruder. Likewise, if I have a right to physical security, then I may rightfully lock my door, flee from assailants, or strike someone who is about to attack me. Rights are linked with the rightfulness of taking steps to avoid being deprived of whatever I have a right to. So, if I have a right to life, then I have a right to take steps to insure that others do not deprive me of my life. In short, I have a right to defend myself.[2]

This argument takes us part of the way toward the conclusion that killing in self-defense is morally permissible. It does not complete the job because although my rights give me moral permissions to take some steps in their defense, they do not permit me to do anything whatsoever in defense of my rights. If I know that someone intends to trespass on my property, there are limits to what I may do to prevent this. I cannot, for example, drop a bomb on the bus that he is taking to my neighborhood. Even though I am defending something to which I have a legitimate right, such a drastic means of defense would be unjustified. The result of defending my rights in this way would be much worse than the invasion of rights which I am trying to prevent.[3]

It is wrong to think, then, that anything goes, so long as it is intended to defend legitimate rights. This makes it possible for the pacifist to maintain that deliberate killing is so dreadful that it cannot be morally justified, even when it is done to protect someone's right to life.

In order to show that killing in defense of oneself or another is morally justified, we must show that it does not exceed the bounds of what is permissible. We must show that it is not like the case of bombing the bus carrying the would-be trespasser, and this does not seem difficult to do. When one person kills another in self-defense, he does not, in protecting his life, cause something which is worse than what would occur if this right were violated. In saying this, I am assuming that it is the attacker alone who will be killed. If defending oneself required killing many innocent people along with the attacker, then matters would be different. But in the case where only the attacker will be killed, the situation one causes in defending one's right is not worse than the situation which would occur if one's right were violated. In either case, one person will be dead, either the attacker or the intended victim. There is no way to prevent both deaths. One person will die, and the choice concerns which one.

Since one person is bound to die, it seems preferable that it be the person who initiated the attack, rather than the victim. The attacker violates the initial presumption against violence, and in doing so, he becomes a legitimate target in a way in which the intended victim is not. The attacker still does have a right to life, since the victim cannot legitimately kill him if there are other less destructive ways of warding off the attack. Nonetheless, by attacking, this person has created a situation in which some life will be lost, and it is better that the life of the attacker be lost than that of the intended victim. So the pacifist is wrong in thinking that it will be better if the victim does not defend his rights by killing.

We can summarize the argument against absolute pacifism in this way: Because people have a right to life, they have a right to take protective and defensive measures in defense of their lives, so long as their doing so does not bring about a situation which would be worse than what would occur if the attack succeeded. In the case of killing an attacker, this condition is satisfied.

If absolute pacifism is not acceptable and there are cases of justifiable killing, then one cannot show that the death penalty is wrong simply by appealing to the idea that all deliberate killing of human beings is wrong.

The Burden of Proof

What we have seen so far is that some acts of deliberate killing are morally right. If this is true, then no argument against the death penalty can succeed if that argument requires a categorical rejection of all killing.

In spite of their failure, these first arguments against the death penalty remain important for several reasons. First, they remind us of the moral gravity of acts of killing. Second, they show that the initial burden of proof is always on those who favor some form of killing. If deliberate killing is generally wrong, then an act of killing will be wrong unless one can show it to be a justifiable exception to the general prohibition. Furthermore, anyone seriously committed to respecting life will want to insure that the list of justifications for killing will be as short as possible. We show our respect for life by demanding that the taking of life be permitted only when the most powerful reasons have been offered. Casually adding to the list of justifiable exceptions to this principle is inconsistent with the reverence for life which is expressed by opponents and supporters of the death penalty alike.

It follows from these points that in the debate about the morality of the death penalty, the moral burden of proof rests on death penalty supporters. Politically, of course, the burden will shift, depending on the current state of the law and public opinion. The political burden of proof falls on those who are dissatisfied with the status quo, and opponents of the death penalty now bear that burden because there are many states which permit executions and because approval of this policy is widespread. Nonetheless, from a moral point of view, the initial burden falls on death penalty supporters. It is they who must bear the burden of showing that the use of death as a punishment for murder is morally permissible, that it is not on a par with murder, that it merits inclusion on the list of justifiable exceptions to the general prohibition of killing.

Respecting the Lives of Victims

There is no reason why death penalty supporters should resist my claim about the burden of proof. They agree that taking a human life is a dreadful act and that in most circumstances, it is wrong to kill. That is why they condemn murder. Nonetheless, they believe that when one person has murdered another, the only way that we can show our respect for the life of the victim is by killing the murderer. To do anything less, they say, is to treat the life of the victim in a casual way. We owe it to the victim not to permit the murderer to continue living. The duty to honor the victim overrides the initial presumption against killing and shows why we can include the death penalty on the list of justifiable killings.

We can formulate this argument for the death penalty in the following manner:

1. We ought to show respect for human life.
2. The only way to show respect for the lives of murder victims is by executing those who killed them.
3. Therefore, murderers should be executed by the state.

Like the previous arguments we have considered, this one contains a premise which both sides would accept. This is the first premise, "We ought to show respect for human life." Not surprisingly, once we get beyond this general moral ideal, matters become more controversial.

Let us consider the second premise, according to which the *only* way in which we can show respect for the life of the victim is by executing the person who caused his death. While this may seem plausible to many people, it is in fact false. If we think about the ways in which we show respect for the dead, it becomes clear that the primary ways involve our behavior toward them, their memories, and things which meant a great deal to them during their lives. Thus, when people die, we attempt to give them a "proper burial," and we have ceremonial ways of indicating that their loss is a serious one. We interrupt our normal activities and set aside periods of mourning. We remember them and mark the anniversary of their deaths. We try to care for those they loved or make contributions to causes that they thought were significant.

All of these are standard expressions of respect, and they remain appropriate, whether a person dies of old age, from a disease, in an accident, or as a result of murder. The crucial thing about all these acts is that they are directed toward the person who died and things which were dear to that person. If we do not know who killed a particular victim and are therefore unable to punish anyone, we would not generally think that we had failed to show proper respect for the victim.

Nonetheless, our treatment of other people might express a lack of respect for the victim. It would surely be a sign of disrespect to the life of the victim if one were to applaud or congratulate the killer. So death penalty advocates are correct in thinking that how we treat a murderer is relevant to whether we are showing respect for the life of the victim. They are wrong, however, in thinking that the only way of expressing our respect for the victim is by killing the murderer. What is primarily required is that we express no positive reaction toward the murderer's deed and that we accord the traditional forms of respect toward the victim. There is no inherent reason, however, why respect for the victim requires the death of the murderer.

What is crucial about our treatment of the murderer is that it be a clear indication of our negative feelings about his act. Many acts might be appropriate—curses, name calling, ostracism, banishment, and imprisonment. It is worth remembering that, according to the biblical account, when Cain killed Abel, the punishment for his crime was banishment: "A fugitive and a vagabond shalt thou be in the earth." Moreover, God marked Cain specifically to prevent others from killing him.[4]

I do not offer the biblical story as a model for how we ought to treat murderers. My point is that when we read or hear the story, we are not generally struck with the thought that God's treatment of Cain was inappropriate or showed disrespect for the life of the dead Abel. If death were the uniquely appropriate response to murder, then the treatment of Cain would strike us as odd and distasteful, but this is not the case.

I do not deny that in our anger we might want to see the murderer die, but that is another matter. What we are considering here is an argument from respect for life, not an argument from anger or vengeance. What I have tried to show is that it is simply false that the only way to show respect for a victim's life is by killing the murderer. There are many ways in which that respect can be shown, and the death of the murderer is not required by our general commitment to respecting the value of life.

Protecting the Innocent

There is an even more serious flaw in the argument we have been considering. Even if it were true that killing murderers is the only way to show respect for the lives of murder victims, it still would not follow that murderers ought to be executed by the state. The reason this would not follow is that governments have other obligations as well, and executing murderers as a sign of respect could conflict with these other obligations. In particular, it could conflict with the obligation of the state to protect the lives of innocent persons.

To see how this could happen, imagine a government with very limited resources for determining the identity of murderers. Because its fact-finding capacities are weak, its judgments about the identity of murderers are wrong half the time. (This is discovered retrospectively. After people have been executed, new evidence appears that reveals their innocence.) In such a situation, it would be blatantly immoral to execute those convicted of murder. Why? Because the execution of innocent persons is inconsistent with a proper respect for human life. Even if executing murderers were the best way of showing our respect for murder victims, it would still be wrong to carry out executions in this situation because the cost in innocent lives would be too high.

In this situation, the desire to show a proper respect for human life leads to two conflicting policies. The problem here is rather like that facing death penalty opponents who are motivated by an abhorrence of killing. They want to show respect for life but are forced to see that respect for life may sometimes lead to conflicts in which we must choose between the lives of attackers and the lives of intended victims. Likewise, in the situation I have just described, death penalty advocates are faced with a conflict in which respect for life leads both to a desire to show respect for victims by executing murderers and to a desire to insure that innocent persons will not be executed. In a simpler world, our values would not generate such conflicts, but we do not live in such a world.

Of course, in our world, we hope that our institutions are more reliable than the ones I have described, and one might object by pointing out that we have a jury system and court procedures through which those accused of murder can defend themselves. So, even if there are occasional mistakes, the rate of accuracy will be much higher than the 50 percent level reached in my imaginary society. This reply is correct but irrelevant. I exaggerated the error rate in my example in order to bring out the point that even if showing proper respect for the lives of victims required executing their murderers, it would not follow that the state ought to adopt the death penalty for murder. Why? Because this might conflict with other aspects of the ideal of respect for life and because the state has special obligations to protect innocent lives. If we knew that in showing respect for the victims, the state would inevitably kill some innocent persons, then the state ought not to carry out executions. The protection of innocent human lives is a primary function of the state, while engaging in symbolic acts of respect is at most a desirable but not central governmental function.

I do not want to discuss here how good our legal system is in making accurate determinations of guilt. I merely want to indicate that the obligation to show respect for the dead is not absolute, that it can conflict with the obligation to protect the living, and that it is more important for governments to protect the living than for them to honor the dead. So, if we have to choose between honoring the dead and protecting the living, we should choose to protect the living. To choose for the state to do otherwise is to see it as a religious rather than a civil institution.

The same problem can be seen from a slightly different angle. Some researchers have claimed that executions have a "brutalizing" effect, that they actually lead to an increase in the number of homicides.[5] Suppose that this is true. We would then have a situation in which the acts by which the state expressed respect for the lives of victims were threatening the lives of other innocent citizens. Again, we would have to make a choice. Would we want the government to honor the lives of murder victims even if this resulted in increased loss of life by other citizens? Or would we want the government to protect the lives of citizens even if this resulted in a failure to express its respect for the lives of victims? In this case, I claim that the state would be obligated to put protection of innocent lives first. The state's obligation to protect the lives of citizens outweighs whatever obligation it might have to honor the dead.

I conclude, then, that the argument for the death penalty which is based on the importance of respecting the lives of victims cannot by itself justify the death penalty for murder. This is because executing murderers is not the only way to show respect for victims' lives, and *even if* it were, it would still be wrong to execute murderers if this caused innocent persons to be executed or led to an increase in the number of murder victims. At the least, the advocate of the death penalty must show that innocent persons will not be executed and that executions will not lead to more homicides. The simple argument we have so far considered focuses on just one factor and leaves out other matters of central importance.

Conclusions

In this chapter, I have considered the ways in which both advocates and opponents of the death penalty appeal to the principle of respect for life. I have tried to show that an attitude of respect for life will not by itself yield a conclusion about the death penalty. Respect for life by itself neither forbids nor requires the execution of murderers. Contrary to some of the arguments against the death penalty, some killing is consistent with respect for life. Nonetheless, the burden is on death penalty advocates to show that executions for murder are a justifiable form of killing, and the argument which appeals to respect for the lives of victims fails to do this.

| 2 |

Killing to Protect Life: The Deterrence Argument

ONE OF THE most powerful arguments made by death penalty supporters is based on the idea that the death penalty is a uniquely effective deterrent against murder. In this chapter, I want to examine the deterrence argument in order to see whether it is consistent with moral principles and whether it is supported by factual evidence.

The Moral Force of Deterrence

We have seen that although killing is generally immoral, there are certain kinds of killings which are justifiable, and one of them is killing in self-defense or in defense of others. Executing a murderer is not itself a case of killing in self-defense, but if death penalty advocates could show that the practice of executing murderers strongly resembles defensive killings in morally relevant ways, that would be an argument for including it on our list of justifiable exceptions. In other words, if there is some property possessed by defensive killings which makes these killings morally right and if executing murderers possesses this same property, then executing murderers would likewise be morally right.

When we compare executions with defensive killings, however, a problem arises immediately. A key factor in our judgment that killing in defense of oneself or others is morally justified is that the victim's life is actually saved by killing the attacker. This crucial factor is missing, however, when the death penalty is inflicted, for the victim is already dead, and the execution of his murderer will not restore him to life. It is hard to imagine that anyone would object to the death penalty if it did restore the victim's life, but we know that it does not have this effect.

Even though the execution of a particular murderer will neither prevent the death of the victim nor restore the victim to life, it might prevent other murders and thus prevent the deaths of other victims. This is the deterrence argument. Though we are powerless to restore life to the dead through executing murderers, we can prevent other murders from occurring by imposing this punishment. The death penalty, on this view, is a kind of social self-defense, an act which, like cases of individual self-defense, results in saving the lives of innocent persons.

The deterrence argument is powerful because it stresses the analogy between the death penalty and defensive killings which are widely thought to be legitimate. Moreover, the argument fits in nicely with the widespread and reasonable view that protecting citizens from harmful attack is one of the central functions of government. If it could be shown that the death penalty would save a substantial number of innocent lives and that no lesser punishment would achieve this as well, then there would be a powerful reason for thinking that executing murderers is a justifiable form of killing. In this situation, no one could complain that the death penalty "did no good" or argue that it simply gratified a desire for revenge.

The crucial question at this point, then, is: does the death penalty deter better than other available punishments?

In considering this question, it is important to see that answering it requires a comparison between the effectiveness of the death penalty and other lesser punishments. We need to know whether the death penalty is a *better* deterrent than other punishments. It is not enough to show that the death penalty prevents murders. It must prevent murders better than lesser punishments. If lesser punishments would do as well, then the deterrence argument would fail.

We can see this by returning to the case of self-defense killing. If someone tries to kill me with a knife and I can protect myself by fleeing or getting the weapon from him, then it would be wrong for me to kill him. Killing him is a last resort which is justified only when it is necessary for saving my life.

Likewise, the deterrence argument justifies the death penalty only if we have no alternative, less extreme punishment which saves lives equally well. I doubt that anyone would deny that the death penalty deters some murderers, if this means only that fewer murders would occur in a situation where the death penalty was imposed than in a situation in which murderers suffered no punishment at all. By itself, however, this is no argument for the death penalty because the same could be said of heavy fines or even short prison sentences. Any of these would have some deterrent force.

Our question, then, is whether the death penalty is a more effective deterrent than lesser punishments and thus saves more lives. Proponents of the death penalty often claim that it is the best deterrent, but we need to see whether their view is supported by the evidence available to us. The most commonly discussed evidence that is relevant to determining whether executions deter best falls into two categories—common sense psychological claims and statistical studies of the impact of executions on homicide rates. I will consider each of these in turn.

The Fear of Death

The common sense argument that death is the best deterrent rests on the belief that people fear death more than they fear anything else. If this is true, then threatening a person with death will have a greater effect on his behavior than any other threat. In particular, the threat of death is more likely to deter a person from committing murder than the threat of long term imprisonment.

Like many of the beliefs expressed in debates about the death penalty, this one has a great deal of surface plausibility, but a bit of reflection shows it to be unfounded. It is simply false that people fear their own deaths more than they fear anything else. This is not to deny that death is a significant evil, for surely it is that. Death is not the loss of one or two things that matter to us. It brings with it the loss of all experience, the termination of all personal plans and hopes, the extinction of all of our potential. Nonetheless, in spite of the genuine loss which typically comes with death, it is not true that death is feared more than anything else.

There are many examples from ordinary experience that show this. I find the following example particularly telling. During his brief term as President, Gerald Ford was the object of two assassination attempts. These attacks brought forth many calls for the death penalty, and there was much talk about death being the only thing that might deter such attacks. At the same time, there was great concern for Ford's safety, and questions were raised about the advisability of public appearances by the President. Ford, however, refused to stop making appearances in public, saying that he refused to be a "prisoner in the White House."

What does this show us? It shows that Gerald Ford regarded the prospect of being a prisoner in the White House as worse than the prospect of risking his own death. Ford probably thought that it was demeaning for the President of the United States to remain confined to the White House, fearful of emerging in public places. He probably thought that he had an obligation to be visible to the public and that hiding away was inconsistent with being a good president. No one thought his decision odd. He was probably admired for his courage. By his behavior, he showed that he did not fear death more than any other thing and that he would continue trying to be a good president, even if this meant risking his life. If everyone feared death more than anything else, Gerald Ford would not have behaved this way. Moreover, if we genuinely believed that everyone feared death more than all else, we would have expected that Ford would retire to the White House, Camp David, and other safe, secluded spots. Most people, however, were probably unsurprised by Ford's statement.

What is striking about this example is how common this sort of behavior is. It is not presidents alone who run such risks. Any person who runs for high office exposes himself to such attacks. Yet, many people run for the presidency in spite of the risk to their lives.

Indeed, when one begins to think about it, all of us risk our lives on many occasions. Mountain climbers risk their lives for thrill and adventure. Patriots risk their lives for their country. Speeding drivers risk their lives in order to get to their destinations a bit faster. Airplane passengers risk their lives in order to visit distant parts of the world, see friends, or complete business transactions. Cigarette smokers risk their lives for pleasure, relaxation, or just out of habit. If we all feared death more than anything else, we would engage in none of these activities.

But we don't fear death more than anything else. We are willing to risk death for innumerable reasons, ranging from the lofty and momentous to the vile and trivial. People who commit murder are like the rest of us in this respect. If they very much want to kill someone, they may well be willing to risk their own lives to do so.

One might object that when people engage in the activities I have described, they don't expect to die. They may see that there is a risk, but they don't really expect death to result from their actions. If they really expected to die as a result of their actions, they would not engage in them. The lesson to be learned, according to this objection, is that if we could administer the death penalty effectively, then prospective murderers would know that if they choose to kill, their own deaths would result. If the death penalty were properly administered and potential murderers faced the certainty of their own deaths rather than a minimal risk of dying, then they would refrain from killing.

The problem with this objection is that we cannot guarantee that all murderers will be executed. Some will not be found out. Some will be tried but acquitted. Some will be found guilty of lesser charges. Some will have their sentences commuted or reversed on appeal. At best, we can increase the probability that murderers will be executed, but it is mere fantasy to expect that we can make execution certain. The result is that someone who wants to kill will be faced with the risk of death and not the certainty of death. There is no way that we can transform this risk into a certainty. Like the rest of us, prospective murderers will often choose to take that risk.

It is worth noting, too, that even if people did fear death more than anything else, that would not establish that death was necessary for deterring people from committing murder. Lesser punishments might be feared enough to have the desired deterrent effect. All of us fear ten years in prison more than one year in prison, but the threat of a one year prison sentence would be quite enough to deter us from parking meter violations. The extra severity is unnecessary for insuring adequate compliance. Likewise, for most of us, the prospect of life imprisonment (or even five or ten years in prison) is so dreadful that increasing the penalty for murder from life imprisonment to death would not provide any additional discouragement. Even if death is more feared than imprisonment, it might well be that long-term imprisonment would deter as well as death. The added severity might not save additional lives.

We can see, then, that the deterrence argument based on the "common-sense" belief that people fear death more than anything else fails. It fails because it does not show either that the threat of death is sufficient to deter murders or that it is necessary to deter murders. What is surprising about the argument is that one continues to hear it and that people take it as obvious, in spite of the fact that it is inconsistent with so much of what we know about our own behavior and the behavior of others around us.

Again, none of this should suggest that death is not a great evil for most of us. It is a significant evil, but for a variety of reasons, we frequently do not take seriously the risks involved in our actions, and this results in our not being deterred from acting in ways which make death more likely.

Systematic Studies of Deterrence

The "common-sense" arguments about deterrence that I have discussed are based on psychological assumptions about attitudes and motivation. They fail because they do not take account of the fact that the death penalty brings with it only a risk of death and not a certainty. The motivational impact of this risk is much weaker than the impact of certain death. Likewise, they fail because they neglect the extent to which people are powerfully motivated by considerations other than those bearing on life and death.

In trying to estimate the deterrent force of the death penalty, as compared with other punishments, one might decide to leave behind assumptions about psychological motivation and try to examine instead the actual effects of imposing or not imposing the death penalty. If proponents of the deterrence argument are correct that the death penalty reduces killings and therefore saves lives, then it is reasonable to expect that fewer people will be murdered in areas where the death penalty has been adopted and that more people will be murdered in areas where there is no death penalty. We can test the deterrent argument, then, by seeing whether more murders occur when people face the possibility of life imprisonment as the maximum sentence and whether fewer murders occur when people are threatened with the possibility of execution.

While this appears to be a straightforward factual matter, the task of actually determining the effect of a particular punishment is quite difficult. The difficulties arise because there are many factors that influence the number of homicides that occur in an area. One may easily be led to believe that a punishment is having a significant influence when no real influence exists. To see this, imagine a case in which a large number of fatal traffic accidents leads to stiffer penalties for speeders. Imagine further that the accident rate declines significantly after the adoption of the new penalties. Can we say that this results from the stiffer penalties? Not really. People's driving habits may have been altered by the mere knowledge of the previous accidents. Frightened by the fatalities, drivers may simply have become more careful, thus bringing the decline in accidents.

What this example shows is that we cannot conclude that a penalty has worked simply because the actions it seeks to prohibit decline when it is imposed. Other factors may have led to the decline. Likewise, even if the penalty did not diminish the number of accidents and fatalities, this would not show conclusively that it had failed to work. It might be that the number of accidents would have risen at an even higher rate if the new penalty had not been enacted. In such a case, the new penalty would have had an effect, but it would not have been powerful enough to counteract other factors and produce a decline in the number of accidents.[1]

Once one recognizes that decreases in crimes do not by themselves show that a more severe punishment is working and that increases in crimes do not show that a more severe punishment is failing to work, one may quickly despair of ever knowing just what the effect of particular punishments is. Many people have adopted just this "we'll never know" attitude toward the deterrence question.

Some researchers, however, have attempted to study the deterrent power of the death penalty in ways that avoid these pitfalls. Methodological problems of the sort I have described are not peculiar to this problem. They occur in many areas of research. Similar difficulties arise, for example, in medical research concerning the causes of disease or the effectiveness of treatments. It is easy to make mistaken inferences about these matters. Nonetheless, when problems are important, we try to overcome the obstacles as best we can, rather than simply give up.

Whether a particular study successfully avoids the problem of mistaking mere correlations for real causes often raises difficult technical problems that lie beyond the competence of people who are untrained in statistical research methods. Those of us who are not specialists have to be cautious and recognize our limitations in considering such issues. Nonetheless, it is important for us to go as far as we can in applying our own wits to understanding them. With this aim in mind, I will describe some of the main studies that have been done on the deterrent power of the death penalty and will indicate some of their strengths and weaknesses. The question of deterrence is so important that these problems cannot be avoided by anyone wishing to form reasonable opinions about the death penalty.

Sellin's Comparisons

One influential set of studies was conducted by Thorstein Sellin. Sellin's basic strategy was to compare homicide rates in two kinds of states, those that did have death penalty statutes and those that did not, in order to see whether homicide rates were lower in states where potential murderers faced the threat of death and higher in states where murderers faced only possible imprisonment. He attempted to avoid the problem of misleading correlations by comparing states which were geographic neighbors and which were similar in many respects. If one could find states which were very similar in many respects and which differed only in their policies toward the death penalty, then comparing them would provide a good test of the effectiveness of the death penalty in saving lives.

Examining homicide rates for the period 1920–1958, Sellin considered eighteen states, grouping them into six clusters, each of which contained three states. The matched groups consisted of states which differed in their punishment policies but which were geographic neighbors and which were "as alike as possible in all other respects—character of population, social and economic condition, etc."[2] While Sellin found that there were regional differences in homicide rates, he did not find any systematic differences in homicide rates between those states which had retained the death penalty and those which had abolished it. In almost every case, abolitionist states had homicide rates that were either lower than or similar to the homicide rates in death penalty states.[3]

The following table represents some of Sellin's findings.[4] In each case, the figure indicates the average annual number of homicides per 100,000 people during the period 1920-1955. States that had death penalty statutes are indicated by a "D".

Michigan 4.8	Minnesota 2.2	N. Dakota 1.4
Indiana (D) 4.8	Wisconsin 1.8	S. Dakota (D)1.6
Ohio (D) 6.1	Iowa (D) 1.7	Nebraska (D) 2.7

Maine 1.6	Rhode Island 1.7
New Hampshire (D) 1.3	Massachusetts (D) 1.7
Vermont (D) 1.2	Connecticut (D) 2.3

Looking at these figures, we can see why Sellin concluded that the death penalty is not a better deterrent of homicides than imprisonment.

Sellin bolstered his conclusion by studying the yearly trends in homicide rates in the matched states, and while there were variations from year to year, the overall trends within each region were quite similar. Sellin took this as an indication that changes in homicide rates resulted from factors other than the death penalty.[5] In addition, since the death penalty is often promoted as a special defense for police officers, he studied attacks on police officers in death penalty and abolition states and concluded that police officers in abolition states were no more likely to be killed than officers in death penalty states.[6]

Sellin's studies are impressive, and they are certainly sufficient to meet the argument of people who believe that the presence or absence of the death penalty by itself has extreme effects on the number of people murdered. Nonetheless, they have been questioned. Perhaps the key criticisms are, first, that the clusters of states which he compared may be different in important respects, even though they are geographic neighbors and share some features, and second, that the mere presence of the death penalty does not deter if there are very few actual executions. In many of the states studied, there were in fact very few executions. Critics of Sellin could claim, with some plausibility, that a death penalty which is "on the books" but which is never administered is the equivalent of no death penalty at all.

Ehrlich's Analysis

While Sellin's work remains one of the most important studies of the impact of the death penalty, the more recent focus of discussion and controversy has been the work of Isaac Ehrlich. Ehrlich is an economist whose application of techniques of economic analysis to the death penalty problem led him to conclude that each execution might be responsible for the prevention of eight deaths by murder.[7]

Ehrlich's analysis has drawn much attention for a number of reasons. First, it was the first systematic study which appeared to support the superior deterrent force of the death penalty. Second, it applied newer and more sophisticated statistical techniques to the deterrence issue, and third, it seems to have influenced the thinking of some Supreme Court justices in their decision to reinstate the death penalty in the 1976 case *Gregg v. Georgia.*

Ehrlich thought that Sellin's study was weakened by the fact that it focused only on whether the death penalty was on the books in particular states. Since executions were very rare in many of these states, it would be a mistake to think that the death penalty was in effect but not working. Instead, one might conclude, it could not deter because it was not a genuine threat. Ehrlich tried to measure the effectiveness of the death penalty by correlating homicide rates with the number of actual executions rather than with laws on the books.

In his study, Ehrlich used figures for executions and murders throughout the United States from 1932–1970 in order to determine the relationship between the frequency of executions and the frequency of homicides. Because the homicide rate is affected by many factors, he constructed an elaborate mathematical formula whose purpose was to allow him to weed out the influence of other factors and so to make a judgment about the degree of influence exercised by the use of the death penalty. Ehrlich's formula represents the homicide rate as a function of several factors: the probability of a murderer being caught, the probability of his being convicted if he is caught, the probability of his being executed if he is convicted, the unemployment rate, the percentage of adults employed, per capita income levels, and the proportion of the population between fourteen and twenty-four years old. Through statistical analysis, Ehrlich thought he could pin down just how much the homicide rate was affected by the probability of execution. He concluded that there was a significant effect—about eight murders were prevented by each execution.

Evaluating Ehrlich's research raises an enormous number of problems, some of which can be assessed only by people with mathematical sophistication and training in social scientific research. Many people with this sort of expertise have rejected his findings. A panel set up by the National Research Council commissioned a study of the Ehrlich findings by Lawrence Klein, holder of the Nobel Prize in Economics for 1980, and two associates. Based on the Klein study, the panel concluded that "the available studies provide no useful evidence on the deterrent effect of capital punishment."[8] While many of the criticisms of Ehrlich's study are quite technical, others can be understood and appreciated by nonexperts.

It is clear that if Ehrlich was to succeed in measuring the effect of executions, he needed to identify correctly the main variables that affect the homicide rate and then use statistical techniques to isolate the amount of the effect due to any single variable. His result would not hold if he failed to include variables which significantly affect homicide rates. David Baldus and James Cole argue that Ehrlich did omit important variables, citing such factors as the rate of migration from rural to urban areas, the rate of weapons ownership among the population, and the rate at which violent crimes other than murder were occurring.[9] Since it is plausible to believe that these factors influence the homicide rate and since Ehrlich's formula omitted them, his analysis could make it appear that changes in the homicide rate were caused by executions when in fact they resulted from these omitted variables.

Other critics question the form in which relevant variables are measured by Ehrlich. To give one example, one of the factors included in Ehrlich's formula is the proportion of the population between ages fourteen and twenty-four. According to Peter Passell and John Taylor, Ehrlich would have gotten a different result if he had included the eighteen to twenty-four year old group rather than the fourteen to twenty-four year olds. The point of including the size of the under twenty-four age group as a factor is that violent behavior is more prevalent among the younger part of the population. Nonetheless, the extreme violence which causes deaths is more plausibly linked to those over eighteen and not to those between fourteen and seventeen.[10]

In addition, unlike Sellin, Ehrlich studied the number of executions and homicides for the United States as a whole, rather than focusing on particular states or regions. This means that if there were significant variations among different regions, these would not be revealed by Ehrlich's study. To take an extreme case, if homicide rates had gone down drastically in nondeath penalty states and risen sharply in death penalty states, Ehrlich's figures would not reveal this. Both his data and his conclusions deal only with the overall rate for the entire United States. For his results to stand up, they need to be corroborated by studies of smaller units. Peter Passell carried out state-by-state analyses of the relationship between executions and homicide rates, using methods similar to Ehrlich's. Analyzing data on forty-one states in 1950 and forty-four states in 1960, he found no deterrent effect of the sort Ehrlich claimed exists.[11]

A final powerful criticism of Ehrlich's finding is that although his study covers a long period of time, 1932-1970, the apparent deterrent force of the death penalty emerges only as a result of homicide and execution rates after 1962. In other words, if one considers only the period up to 1962, Ehrlich's striking result does not emerge. One would think that if the death penalty exercised a steady influence on homicides, then there would be no difference if a few years were dropped from the sample, yet this is not so. The omission of the years from 1962 to 1970 has a drastic effect on Ehrlich's result.

Moreover, it is easy to account for the change which occurs after 1962. Starting at that point, the attack on capital punishment in the courts was leading to a radical drop in the number of executions. Likewise, beginning in 1965, there was a tremendous surge in the homicide rate. The result is that murders increased while executions decreased. This set of events in the 1960s is responsible for most of the effect which Ehrlich's analysis purports to find operating through the earlier decades.[12]

These criticisms strike me as being quite forceful and, in my judgment, they effectively undermine Ehrlich's alleged vindication of the superior deterrent force of the death penalty.

Killing to Protect Life: The Deterrence Argument

The 1960s: Rising Crime and the Judicial Moratorium

Although the dramatic drop in executions and the rise in homicides during the 1960s may diminish the force of Ehrlich's research, it nonetheless may appear to furnish those who believe in deterrence with a powerful argument. From their perspective, what they see is a huge rise in the number of murders following right upon a cessation of executions. It appears obvious to them that the moratorium on executions caused the increase in the homicide rate. Discussing this period, Frank Carrington writes that criminals "were actually taking advantage of the efforts of abolitionists," and he claims that "statistics seem to bear . . . out" this conclusion. He offers the following chart as evidence:[13]

Year	Number of Executions	Number of Homicides
1955	76	7,000+
1960	56	8,000+
1966	1	10,000+
1972	0	18,000+
1975	0	20,000+

While these statistics are both accurate and dramatic, they do not in fact bear out Carrington's conclusion that the increase in homicides resulted from the decrease in executions.

What is the matter with Carrington's inference? First, it neglects the fact that many things (other than the decline in executions) were going on during the period shown on the chart. Passell and Taylor, discussing the period 1963–1969, mention the lower cost and greater availability of weapons, increased racial tension, a general reduction in the severity of prison sentences, and an increased gap between people's economic expectations and their actual economic status. Another factor frequently mentioned is the effect of the postwar baby boom, which resulted in a great increase in the size of the most violent group within society, males between eighteen and twenty- five years old.

More careful studies reveal other facts which undermine Carrington's simple correlation. While the homicide rate did increase, it increased at a much slower rate than other crimes, which really did skyrocket during this period. Since the death penalty had never been a factor in these other crimes, its absence could not have accounted for their increase. Yet it is plausible that whatever forces led to the general increase were likewise responsible for the rise in homicides as well.

Finally, comparative studies have been done for this period of homicide rates in states which had the death penalty and those which lacked it. If the growth in homicides were caused by the absence of the death penalty, one would expect that the increase in homicides would occur in death penalty states. It is death penalty states which suddenly found themselves without the ability to threaten execution, while this threat had never been a factor in abolitionist states. In fact, this is not what happened. Using a matching comparative method like that of Sellin, William Bowers found that in some cases, there were greater increases in homicides in abolitionist states than in former death penalty states. In other cases, the two kinds of states increased in parallel fashion. Overall, however, there was no evidence that death penalty states experienced greater increases as a result of the moratorium and their inability to execute murderers.[14] There is no reason, then, to believe that the temporary absence of executions caused the increase in homicides that occurred after 1965. These developments do not support Carrington's claims on behalf of the deterrent power of the death penalty.

Brutalization and the Counterdeterrent Effect

In thinking about the effects of the death penalty, it is important to consider one possibility that would totally undermine the common belief in the protective powers of executions. This is the idea that executions actually cause homicides and thereby lead to an increase in homicide rates. Belief in this counterdeterrent effect is often called the "brutalization hypothesis," and several researchers have claimed that this hypothesis has strong empirical support. Brutalization theorists believe that executing murderers both legitimates killing as a means of dealing with conflict and also stimulates those who have violent tendencies.

Studies in support of the brutalization hypothesis generally focus on relatively short term effects, in an attempt to gauge the impact of individual executions. The most extensive study of this sort has been carried out by William Bowers and Glen Pierce, who examined monthly records of executions and homicides in New York State from 1907 through 1964. During the period studied, New York had more homicides than any other state and executed more murderers than any other state. The Bowers and Pierce study, then, covers a long period of time and focuses on a state where there were many executions. Using various statistical techniques to isolate seasonal variations in homicide rates, they concluded that if one or more executions occurred in a given month, an average of two additional homicides would occur during the following month.[15] Moreover, Bowers and Pierce claim that when the method employed by Ehrlich is properly carried out, it also reveals a brutalizing rather than a deterrent effect on homicides.[16]

If this conclusion is correct, its implications for the death penalty debate are doubly powerful. First, it undermines the belief in the superior deterrence of the death penalty and thereby refutes the moral argument based on the analogy with defensive killing. Second, it provides a strong reason for rejecting any nondeterrence kind of argument for executions by showing that even if other goals might be achieved by executions, it would be at the cost of innocent lives.

Special Deterrence

Before concluding, we should turn briefly to another kind of deterrence argument. The argument we have so far considered involves "general deterrence," the idea that by punishing one person, we discourage others from committing crimes. Some arguments, however, focus on "special deterrence," preventing a person who has already violated the law from committing additional crimes. Sometimes this effect of punishment is called "incapacitation."

According to the special deterrence argument for the death penalty, we ought to execute a person who commits murder because that is the surest way of preventing that person from murdering again.

This argument rests on a proposition that no one would deny: Murderers who have been executed will not commit additional murders. The truth of this statement, however, is not enough to make the argument succeed. As we noted earlier, the analogy with killing in self-defense requires that killing to save lives is justified only if there is no less severe action which would have the same effect. In this case, however, life imprisonment would provide the same protection to society that execution does. It would isolate convicted murderers and thus deprive them of further opportunities to kill innocent citizens.

Of course, imprisonment will not achieve these ends as perfectly as executions, since there is a chance that murderers may escape, be released, or kill while in prison. In this sense, death penalty advocates are correct in arguing that executing a murder is the most effective special deterrent. Nonetheless, imprisonment goes a long way toward meeting their goal. In order to see whether imprisonment is successful enough, we have to see just how great a threat is posed by convicted murderers.

Hugo Bedau has compiled statistics concerning the number of homicides committed by people who were previously convicted of murder. His study covers twelve states from 1900 to 1976. Of the 2,646 people convicted of murder and subsequently released from prison, only sixteen were subsequently convicted of homicide. Later nationwide studies for 1965–1974 show that of 11,404 people convicted of willful homicide and released from prison, thirty-four committed murder in the year following release from prison. It may well be that these people ought not to have been released, but in any case the number who commit additional killings is quite small. In order to prevent a small number of killings, one would have to execute thousands of convicted murderers. Most of those who commit murder will not repeat their crime, and society can gain additional protection through more stringent release policies rather than executions.[17]

Finally, it is worth noting the claim that the death penalty provides additional protection to prison guards and officials since it deters those in prison already from committing murder. Wendy Wolfson reviewed records of prison homicides and found, first, that most victims of prison homicides are inmates rather than officials; second, that most prison homicides are committed by people convicted of crimes other than murder; and finally, that prison homicides do not occur less frequently in death penalty states.[18] There is no evidence to support the claim, then, that prison officials would be better protected if the death penalty were carried out for convicted murderers. Even this more restricted version of the deterrence argument is unsupported by the available evidence.

Conclusions

Most people begin with a strong conviction that the death penalty will deter murders more effectively than long-term imprisonment. Moreover, to many, this belief seems not only to be true—it seems to be obviously true. Yet, we have seen that there are many reasons for rejecting it. At the level of common sense psychology, reflections on people's behavior suggest that the fear of death is less powerful a motive than one might think. When we look to statistical studies aimed at showing the relationship between executions and homicide rates, there appears to be a consensus among the experts that Ehrlich's study was flawed and that researchers have been unable to find that executions prevent homicides. Moreover, studies by Sellin and others provide some positive evidence against the deterrence thesis and even some reason to believe that the death penalty may cause additional murders.

What conclusion should we draw then? Several different conclusions from the data are possible. The most startling conclusion is that the death penalty actually causes homicides. A less surprising but still significant view is that executions simply do not deter better than other severe punishments. A still more limited claim is that while there is no strong evidence for the superior deterrent power of the death penalty, the evidence available does not show that it fails to deter best. Finally, one might conclude that we just do not know and cannot know whether the death penalty saves lives.

I believe that there is a basis for a confident rejection of the deterrence thesis, but even the more cautious and limited conclusion that the deterrent effect has not been proved is sufficient for undermining the deterrence argument. The death penalty can be justified as analogous to defensive killing only if it can be shown that it does save lives. Since that has not been shown, one cannot appeal to this protective function as providing a moral basis for executing murderers. Despite the initial moral force of the deterrence argument, its factual presupposition—that the death penalty saves lives— is not sufficiently supported by available evidence. The deterrence argument fails to justify the death penalty.

| 3 |

The Economic Argument for Executions

THE ECONOMIC ARGUMENT for executions is simple and direct. It costs much more to imprison murderers for life than it does to execute them. Therefore, we ought to execute them.

Stated in this manner, the economic argument seems to reveal a disturbing lack of moral sensitivity. For this reason, the argument does not usually appear in written defenses of the death penalty. Nonetheless, in my experience, it almost always emerges in informal discussions of the death penalty. While some people may consider it beneath comment, I think it unwise to ignore the argument. We can learn some important lessons by considering it.

Cost Savings and the Value of Life

Whatever its force, the argument is something of an embarrassment to death penalty advocates. If a moral argument is to be made for the death penalty, then it must be shown that use of the death penalty is consistent with a high regard for the value of human life. The economic argument does not appear consistent with that high regard, and so it threatens to reveal death penalty supporters as callous and insensitive. This is an important point because the moral credibility of a position is undermined if it appears that one has to be callous to hold it. To retain credibility, both sides have to display a high degree of concern and respect for the value of human life.

On behalf of those who use the economic argument, it is worth remembering that there are many situations in which people must consider the cost of saving human lives. This is done when we decide whether to make expensive medical treatments freely available to all. It is done when airlines or auto manufacturers make decisions about the safety of their products. While these decisions are not always made in a morally conscientious manner and sometimes do display callous disregard for human life, one must acknowledge that there is a limit to the sacrifices people are willing to make in order to save human lives. We know that we could save many lives by closing down highways and trading in our cars for bicycles. Yet, we do not make this decision because it would be too costly. It would deprive us of many benefits, both economic and noneconomic. So, lives are weighed and balanced against other goods, and we do not think that all who engage in this sort of deliberation are necessarily without conscience or moral sensitivity.

Having said this, however, I think the most important defense of the integrity of those who raise the economic argument for executions is that they don't really mean it. They are not genuinely committed to the idea that we ought to execute murderers because it is cheaper than imprisoning them.

We can see this by asking whether those who support executing murderers on economic grounds would also favor executing car thieves, embezzlers, tax evaders, blackmailers, drug users, and others who are currently imprisoned. If one favored executing murderers rather than imprisoning them *simply* because executions are less costly than imprisonment, then one would have to favor executing *all* those who commit crimes for which imprisonment is the usual punishment because this would be more economical. Yet, few if any people would favor such an extreme policy.

My point here is that if people were really motivated by the economic argument alone, they would favor the death penalty for a whole range of crimes, many of which are less serious than murder. Since people do *not* favor the death penalty for these other crimes, it is clear that the low cost of executions is not really what is behind their argument. If we were to ask why car thieves, tax evaders, and others convicted of crimes ought not to be executed—even though it would be cheaper than imprisoning them—the answer would be that they do not *deserve* such a terrible punishment, whereas murderers do. Since murderers deserve to die anyway, there is nothing wrong with saving money by taking their lives.

When I said, then, that proponents of the economic argument

did not really mean it, what I meant was that they were not really proposing to execute murderers just because this was cheaper. The economic argument really rests on the more basic claim that murderers deserve to die. I believe that almost everyone who raises the economic argument does so on the assumption that it is morally right to kill murderers because they deserve it. Without that assumption, these people would be embarrassed to argue from economy.

If my account is correct, then few people support executions just because they are cheaper. Rather, they think it is permissible to save money by executing murderers because they think that murderers deserve to die anyway. In later chapters, I will consider the argument that we ought to execute murderers because they deserve to die. At this point, I would like to pursue the economic argument, even though few people would support it in its pure form.

In studying and analyzing arguments, we frequently find that different arguments become entangled with one another. Arriving at a clear understanding of them requires separating them and looking at each one by itself. Having distinguished the economic argument from its frequent unstated companion, the argument from desert, we can see how much force the economic argument has.

The Real Costs of Executions

Like the deterrence argument, the economic argument rests on a set of factual assumptions. In this case, the assumptions concern the relative costs of executing people as opposed to imprisoning them for a long period of years. It seems obvious that executions are less costly. It does not cost very much to give a person a lethal injection, shoot several bullets in him, poison him with gas, or electrocute him. On the other hand, imprisonment means paying for the prisoner's food, clothing, and shelter, as well as for the guards and other officials required for his care. If we multiply the annual cost of maintaining a person in prison by the number of years he spends there, we would expect to arrive at a rather large figure. It seems difficult to avoid the conclusion that it costs more to imprison someone for long periods than it does to execute him.

While this conclusion looks very plausible, it is in fact false. In order to assess the true costs of the death penalty, we cannot just compare the costs of confining one person with the costs of executing him. Rather we must consider the costs of maintaining the whole set of institutions that surround the death penalty. When we take this broader perspective, we will see that the costs of imposing the death penalty are in fact greater than the costs of imprisonment.

In an informative article on "The Cost of Capital Punishment," Barry Nakell explains why the costs of executions are greater than one might think.[1] To begin with, the trial process is more costly when death is a possible punishment. While most criminal cases are resolved by guilty pleas and thus do not require a trial, all capital cases require a jury trial, and these trials tend to be longer, more complex, and more costly than other trials. Selection of juries takes longer, and questions concerning the sanity of the defendant are more likely to be raised, requiring expert testimony and longer deliberations. Once a person is convicted, a separate sentencing hearing must be held, and a wide variety of witnesses and information will be brought in if the defense has the resources to try to establish mitigating factors in the defendant's background.

If a death sentence is handed down, the chance of the case being appealed is greatly increased. In most states, automatic reviews by state supreme courts are required by death penalty legislation. Frequently, retrials are required because so much is at stake that technical errors have increased importance. Because most defendants in murder cases are poor and because the costs of legal defense are so heavy, the state pays not only for court officials and prosecutors but often for defense attorneys too.

Finally, even within prisons, extra facilities are required, including apparatus for the execution and specially secure "death row" areas. Because of long appeals processes, inmates on death row may spend many years receiving this specially expensive care. After all this, many defendants will not ultimately be executed.

Nakell gives a good overview of the reasons why capital cases are more expensive. Other studies are more specific in giving costs. In a recent study of legal costs in California, Margot Garey notes that while jury selection takes an average of three days in noncapital cases, it consumes an average of sixteen days in capital cases. Since operating a courtroom costs about $2,200 per day, the jury selection process alone will cost on the average almost $30,000 more in capital cases.[2] Once the jury is selected, the trial procedure is also longer, averaging forty-two days in capital cases, as opposed to twelve days in noncapital cases. Each additional day increases not only the courtroom costs but also the costs of both prosecutors and defense attorneys.[3] The trial is then followed, in cases of conviction, by the sentencing hearing, which is in many ways a second trial, as well as by subsequent reviews and appeals, all of which are required because of the severity and finality of the punishment in this type of case.

I will not try to summarize all of the data presented in Garey's study. Her report lends credence to some of the estimates others have given in speaking of the financial burden of the death penalty system. A 1982 report by the New York State Defenders Association concluded that it would cost the state of New York more than $1.4 million to conduct the legal processes required for executing a single person, along with an additional $330,000 for appeals costs.[4] In New Jersey, it was estimated that a new death penalty law would cost the state an additional $16 million per year.[5] In 1970, when the state of Arkansas commuted the death sentences of fifteen inmates, the savings in appeals costs alone were estimated at $1.5 million.[6]

All of these figures support Nakell's judgment that

> although it may cost less to execute a particular prisoner than to maintain him for life, it costs far more to finance a system by which we decide to execute some people and end up still maintaining for life many of the people processed through that system.[7]

The key word here is "system." When we think about the death penalty, we are tempted to think of the isolated execution of a particular individual. The execution itself is a brief event and appears to require few resources. In fact, however, the death penalty is part of a complex legal structure, and so the existence of the death penalty brings with it implications for the legal system. When we consider the financial costs of the death penalty, we need to keep in mind that we are evaluating a system. Otherwise, we will neglect many important features of the death penalty, and we will underestimate the financial costs of maintaining it. Once we recognize these wider institutional costs, it becomes clear that the death penalty is no bargain.

Cutting Judicial Costs

At this point, death penalty proponents may express some impatience with the argument, for it is not the actual executions that are costly. We know that people can be killed cheaply. Rather, the high costs result from the elaborate legal processing of cases. Since many people are impatient with legal "technicalities" and "excessive" procedures anyway, the suggestion may be made that we can decrease the cost of the death penalty by curtailing the judicial processing that surrounds it.

Here again, death penalty advocates need to proceed with care if they are to argue for executions without violating the deep respect for human life which they say motivates them. Anyone who cares about justice and respect for human life will want to be very certain that innocent persons are not punished. The jury system and the system of appeals exist to make sure that anyone who is subject to criminal punishment has the best chance to defend himself, either by establishing his innocence or by showing that a lesser rather than a greater punishment is more just in his situation. If we curtail the judicial processes available to a person charged with a crime, we deprive him of the opportunity to protect himself from unjust punishment.

In addition, the more severe are the potential punishments facing an individual, the more important are the procedural safeguards and other legal devices whose purpose it is to insure that justice is done. Since death penalty advocates support the most severe punishment, they are under a special obligation to support a legal process which will filter out the innocent and treat the guilty justly and equitably.

The need for legal appeals and other safeguards varies directly with the severity of possible punishments. Where mild punishments are involved, we do not feel the same need for safeguards. In the case of a traffic violation, for example, I may have few options, even if I am innocent, but we do not think this is a grave injustice because the typical punishments are quite limited. If, however, we are considering putting people in prison for a substantial period or depriving them of life entirely, then we must give them every benefit of the doubt. To do otherwise is to show a callous disregard for human life and well-being. For these reasons, death penalty advocates ought not to be in the position of calling for both the most extreme of penalties and the lessening of legal safeguards for persons accused of crimes.[8]

Due Process Costs and the "Veil of Ignorance"

In thinking about the value of legal safeguards for people accused of crimes, it is easy for us to be overly influenced by our own particular situation. Most of us do not expect to murder anyone. Nor do we expect to be accused of murder or other serious crimes. We may therefore see procedural safeguards solely as impediments to effective law enforcement and as costly excesses which show too much concern for the well-being of criminals. We fail to recognize their value as guarantors of human rights and human well-being.

For these reasons, it is sometimes helpful to change our perspective when we consider whether particular institutions should be adopted or altered. In *A Theory of Justice*, the philosopher John Rawls has suggested that one way to determine whether the basic institutions of society are just is to consider whether we would agree to them if they were presented to us as part of a social contract. Furthermore, in considering these institutions, we are to imagine that we are behind what Rawls calls a "veil of ignorance."[9] That is, we are to imagine that, in making our choices, we do not know just who we are in society or what our social position is. Given this ignorance, we are forced to consider that we might occupy any position within society. A just institution is one which we would accept no matter what social position we ended up occupying.

Applying this perspective to the issues at hand, we can ask ourselves two questions. First, would we want to live in a society where the decision to execute people was made on the basis of economy? Second, would we want to live in a society where severe punishments, including execution, were imposed and where there were limited opportunities for establishing one's innocence or contesting the justice of a particular punishment? In answering these questions, we need to consider that we might be law-abiding citizens who are never accused of any crime. Or we might be persons (whether guilty or innocent) who are accused of crime and face the possibility of severe punishment, including death.

Consider the first question. Would we favor executing murderers to save money if we were in a position of not knowing whether we were to be accused of murder or not? I think we would oppose economically motivated executions, unless our society was so badly off that innocent people were severely disadvantaged by maintaining prisons for incarcerating criminals. If the society were affluent and only small sacrifices were required, we would not choose to execute people to save money. We would not ourselves want to be executed so that others could share in minor tax savings. Moreover, knowing that death is an irrevocable punishment, we would not want to deprive ourselves of later opportunities for vindicating our innocence, should we find ourselves falsely convicted.

Likewise, if we were in a society which did choose to execute people for murder or other crimes and if we did not know our place in that society, we would want to provide ourselves with adequate protection in case we ourselves were ever accused of a serious crime. Thus, we would sign a social contract only if it provided for such protections as a right of trial, a right to adequate legal representation, and a right to call witnesses. Further, if death were a possible punishment, we would want the right to have our case reviewed by appellate courts to insure that we had been treated in accord with law and had not been victims of hysteria or prejudice. The more severe the punishments that might be meted out upon us, the more would we insist on strong procedural safeguards.

Taking this social contract perspective seems to me to confirm the conclusions I stated earlier. First, it provides additional grounds for rejecting an economic argument—unless the society was in the direst of straits so that maintaining prisoners deprived people of basic needs. Even in this case, if a society were looking for ways of conserving its limited resources, it might well banish or exile criminals rather than execute them. Second, if one is going to impose severe penalties, then both a commitment to justice and a respect for human life require that the system provide processes for defense, redress, and appeal. To cut these aspects of the system while being willing to impose death as a punishment is to fail to respect human life properly. We cannot consistently claim to value and respect human life, while at the same time being willing to curtail legal safeguards which provide essential protections for human life.

Conclusions

We began with an argument for the death penalty which appealed to its economic implications: Because executing murderers is less expensive than imprisoning them for long periods, we ought to execute them. Our examination of this argument revealed a number of defects. First, when we attend to the institutional costs of maintaining the death penalty, it turns out that it is a costly institution. Legal costs are much increased when death is an option, so we do not save money by adopting the death penalty.

Second, if someone were to reply that we could cut costs by curtailing the legal process, this reply shows insufficient regard for the value of human life. The more severe the possible penalties are, the more we are in need of appeals and other costly legal protective devices. Signers of a social contract would insist on these safeguards if their society were to be empowered to administer death as a punishment. Likewise, except possibly in the most severely deprived social situations, they would not permit executions to occur for economic reasons.

Finally, I suggested earlier that most proponents of the economic argument are not callous about the value of human life but are tacitly assuming that the lives of murderers are different, that murderers can legitimately be killed to save money because they deserve to die in any case. Another way of putting this is to say that since murderers deserve to die, we are not required to make any sacrifices to keep them alive. We owe them nothing and thus can justifiably choose to kill them rather than to make any sacrifice on their behalf.

This version of the economic argument presupposes the belief that murderers deserve to die. This belief is one of the most powerful and important ideas in the death penalty debate. It is time to consider whether it provides an adequate basis for supporting the death penalty.

| 4 |

Should We Execute Those Who Deserve to Die?

MANY PEOPLE BELIEVE that murderers deserve to die and therefore that the state ought to execute them. I will call this reasoning
the "argument from desert."

The argument from desert has very broad appeal, and death
penalty opponents need to show that it is mistaken if their position is to be taken seriously. In order to show this, death penalty
opponents must make a convincing case for the truth of at least
one of the following statements:

1. People who commit murder do not deserve to die.
2. Even if people who commit murder deserve to die, it is wrong
   for the state to execute them.

If either one of these statements can be established, then the
argument from desert fails.

I will try to show that *both* of these statements are true and
therefore that the argument from desert does not provide a morally sound justification for the death penalty.

Giving People What They Deserve

In beginning our consideration of the argument from desert, let
us assume that death penalty advocates are correct in asserting
that murderers deserve to die. While it may appear that if we
assume this, then the argument for the death penalty is unstoppa-
ble, this impression is mistaken. There is no inconsistency in
conceding that murderers deserve to die and still opposing the
death penalty. These two beliefs are consistent because there may
be quite good reasons in particular cases why people should not

get what they deserve. This is especially true when the body that is to give someone his just deserts is the government.

One reason for not giving a person what he deserves is that doing so conflicts with other obligations that one has. In chapter 2, I mentioned the brutalization hypothesis, according to which executions actually cause homicides. If this hypothesis is true, it provides the government with a powerful reason not to execute convicted murderers, even if they deserve to die. The reason is that the government's policy of giving murderers their just deserts would be carried out at the cost of having innocent people lose their lives. Faced with a choice between giving murderers what they deserve and protecting innocent lives, the government ought to choose protection of the innocent over execution of the guilty. It is more important to save innocent lives than to terminate guilty ones, and it is a more central function of government that it protect people's well-being than that it carry out the distribution of just deserts.

This example is somewhat hypothetical because the brutalization effect remains controversial and has not yet influenced governmental policy. In any case, there are many ways in which our legal system currently departs from a policy of giving people what they deserve. One such case is the prohibition of double jeopardy. Our system does not permit a person to be tried more than once for a particular crime. If he is tried and acquitted, that is the end of it.

Now imagine a case of a person who has been accused of murder. He is tried and acquitted, and as he leaves the courthouse, he tells reporters, "I did it, and I got away with it." If this person did commit the murder and if murderers deserve to die, then he deserves to die. Nonetheless, the government may not prosecute him again for this charge and may not punish him, even though, from a moral point of view, he deserves to die. In this case, the prohibition on double jeopardy outweighs whatever obligation there might be to give this person what he deserves.

Considering this situation, one could claim, of course, that it shows that the legal system is defective and that we ought to abolish the double jeopardy rule. There are good reasons, however, for retaining the prohibition of double jeopardy. It protects all citizens from continued threats and harassment by government officials. If we could always be brought back for retrial even though we had been acquitted of the crime in question, then we would be continually exposed to threats by unscrupulous officials. The double jeopardy rule provides a significant protection for all citizens, and it is wise to keep the rule, even if this means sometimes failing to give the guilty what they deserve.

If giving people what they deserve were the only function of the legal system, these problems would not arise. The design of our legal system incorporates other aims, however. We have already seen this in discussing the costs of capital punishment and the necessity for procedural safeguards surrounding its use. The effect of these multiple aims is that we must sometimes sacrifice the goal of giving people what they deserve in order to satisfy other goals of greater importance. So, even if one concedes that murderers deserve to die, one need not grant that the government ought to execute them. This is because executing them may conflict with other important goals or ideals.

Death penalty supporters might concede this point in principle but deny that any such conflicts arise with respect to the death penalty. The question we must answer, then, is whether there are significant legal or moral goals and ideals which conflict with the imposition of the death penalty.

Furman v. Georgia

The Eighth Amendment to the United States Constitution prohibits the use of cruel and unusual punishments, and in 1972, the Supreme Court decided that the death penalty, *as it was then administered*, was cruel and unusual.

While each justice wrote a separate opinion in *Furman v. Georgia*, the most significant argument that emerged against the death penalty was based on the view that the death penalty was imposed in an arbitrary manner. In a widely accepted analysis of the Court's action, Charles Black has written:

> The decisive ground of the 1972 Furman case anti-capital punishment ruling—the ground persuasive to the marginal justices needed for a majority—was that, out of a large number of persons "eligible" in law for the punishment, a few were selected as if at random, by no stated (or perhaps statable) criteria, while all the rest suffered the lesser penalty of imprisonment.[1]

In focusing, then, on how the death penalty was administered, the Court was not concerned with whether the actual executions were performed in a cruel and unusual manner. Rather, the justices were concerned with the procedures under which death penalty sentences were being determined, and they judged the punishment to be unacceptable because life and death decisions were being made in an arbitrary way.

In understanding the Court's reasoning, it is important to recall that current laws do not embody the judgment that all people guilty of homicide deserve to die. Some killings are not even called "murder," but are classified as manslaughter, usually because there was no intention to kill. Even among murders, the laws of many states distinguish between first and second degrees of murder. Only those guilty of first degree murder are eligible for the death penalty, and even among these, judges or juries may decide that their crimes were not sufficiently terrible to merit death. The aim of this system of classifications is to select those killings which are the very worst and to impose the death penalty only in these cases. Underlying this system, then, is the judgment that only those guilty of the worst murders deserve to die. Some people who murder deserve a lesser punishment.

The Court's complaint with the administration of the death penalty was that this system of grading punishments according to the crime was not working. Decisions concerning executions were being made arbitrarily and not on the basis of facts about the crime. This was happening because the law contained no clear criteria that juries could apply when deciding which murderers ought to be executed and which ought to be imprisoned. In the absence of clear criteria, these judgments were determined by legally irrelevant factors.

In explaining their positions, different justices on the Court emphasized different forms of arbitrariness. Justice Stewart objected to the random aspects of the sentencing process, explaining his objection as follows:

> These death sentences are cruel and unusual in the same way that being struck by lightning is cruel and unusual. For of all the people convicted of rapes and murders in 1967 and 1968, *many just as reprehensible as these,* the petitioners are among *a capriciously selected random handful* upon whom the sentence has in fact been imposed.[2]

In other words, there was no reasonable basis for the execution of these people and the imprisonment of others. Many were equally reprehensible, and so it was "cruel and unusual" to single out only a few for the severest punishment.

Other justices stressed a fact that had long been emphasized by death penalty opponents, its discriminatory application. According to them, the application of the death penalty was arbitrary but not entirely random. Rather, racial bias created a situation in which blacks were more likely to be executed than whites. In fact, prejudice had a significant double effect on sentencing, since blacks who killed whites were among those most likely to be executed, while whites who killed blacks were the least likely to be sentenced to die.[3] Similarly, economic and social status influenced these judgments in illegitimate ways. These were the arbitrary features stressed by Justice Douglas. As he wrote,

> In a Nation committed to equal protection of the laws there is no permissible "caste" aspect of law enforcement. Yet we know that the discretion of judges and juries in imposing the death penalty enables the penalty to be selectively applied, feeding prejudices against the accused if he is poor and despised, and lacking political clout, or if he is a member of a suspect or unpopular minority, and saving those who by social position may be in a more protected position.[4]

Douglas argued, then, that the death penalty was cruel and unusual because it was applied to people (or not applied to them) for reasons that were legally irrelevant and impermissible. It would violate the Constitution to have a law that permitted the execution only of poor people or members of racial minorities. Since this was how the death penalty was operating in fact, its use under those conditions was unconstitutional.

The Moral Basis of the Furman Decision

In considering these issues, the Supreme Court was treating them as matters of constitutional law. The question facing the Court was whether the arbitrary imposition of the death penalty made it unconstitutional. Nonetheless, the issues involved in the *Furman* case are not solely matters of constitutional law. For opponents of the death penalty, the pattern of arbitrary and discriminatory sentencing is itself a deplorable moral injustice. Even if these practices were permissible under the Constitution, they would still be morally unjust.

I believe that this moral condemnation is appropriate and that the Court's reasoning has moral as well as legal force. The *Furman* argument illuminates the true but paradoxical judgment that it can be morally unjust to punish someone for a crime even if he morally deserves to be punished.

In order to see that it can actually be unjust to give someone what he deserves, imagine a group of fifty people, all of whom have committed dreadful murders. Suppose that each one's act is so horrible that we would have no trouble concluding that each one deserved to die. In spite of this, however, only those with red hair are sentenced to die, while all others are given lesser sentences. In this situation, the red-headed murderers would certainly feel that they were being treated unjustly, and I think that they would be correct.

Even if a person deserves to die, that is not enough to make his execution just. In addition, it is necessary that he be executed *because* he deserves to die. In the case I have described, we cannot explain why the red-headed murderers were sentenced to die by saying that they deserved it. This explanation is insufficient because others who were equally deserving were not sentenced to die. So, if we try to explain the decision to execute some but not others, the explanation would be that they were people with red hair who had committed heinous murders. Yet, it is surely unjust to execute someone *because* he is a red-headed murderer rather than a blond or black-haired murderer. This would be cruel and unusual in the sense stressed by Douglas, since it would involve basing the degree of punishment on features of a person which are irrelevant. It is especially unjust if the punishment is determined by features of a person over which he has little or no control.

Even if we grant, then, that only those who deserve to die are ever sentenced to die, we would be forced to see the death penalty as unjust if its actual imposition depended on such factors as race, economic status, ability to acquire adequate legal representation, or other facts which have nothing to do with a person's culpability. That is the underlying moral argument of the *Furman* decision, and it is a powerful, important moral argument, even apart from its constitutional significance.

Eliminating Arbitrariness

The problem of arbitrariness has been addressed by death penalty supporters in two ways. After the *Furman* decision, state legislatures passed new laws that were designed to eliminate the influence of arbitrary features from death penalty impositions. Two strategies were pursued. In some states, the death penalty was made mandatory for certain types of crimes. Anyone convicted of them would be executed so that both randomness and discrimination could play no role. This strategy was rejected by the Supreme Court. In *Woodson v. North Carolina*, it ruled that mandatory death sentences were unconstitutional, since they failed to permit consideration of individual differences among defendants.[5]

The second legislative strategy was to leave room for judgment but to eliminate arbitrariness by providing specific guidelines for juries to follow in deciding on the appropriate sentence. This is the strategy of "guided discretion," under which the law leaves the final judgment to juries but specifies what kinds of reasons may be used in determining whether a particular murderer ought to be executed or imprisoned. Typically, these guidelines consist of lists of aggravating and mitigating circumstances, features of the crimes or persons that may make the crime worse or less bad. The new laws also included other procedural safeguards, such as automatic appeals or reviews of death sentences and separate sentencing hearings, which allow defendants to present additional factors on their behalf.

In its 1976 decision in *Gregg v. Georgia*, the Supreme Court ruled that statutes incorporating "guided discretion" and other safeguards were constitutional because they made arbitrariness sufficiently unlikely. In making this ruling, the Court did not reject the *Furman* argument that arbitrarily imposed executions are cruel and unusual. Rather, it claimed that arbitrariness had been sufficiently eliminated so as to guarantee fair proceedings and controlled, unbiased sentencing.

The *Gregg* decision has prompted death penalty opponents to argue that "guided discretion" is an illusion and that even under the new laws, sentences in capital cases continue to be arbitrary and discriminatory. I do not at this point want to consider the evidence for these claims. Instead, I simply want to point out that if these claims are correct, then the Court would be bound to return to its earlier judgment that the death penalty was unconstitutional. This is because the Court did not reject the argument that *if* the death penalty is arbitrarily administered, then it violates the Constitution. Instead, it decided that under the new laws, the death penalty would no longer be administered arbitrarily.

Against the Argument from Arbitrariness

Although death penalty supporters have tried to make death sentencing less arbitrary, some of them explicitly reject the use of the argument from arbitrariness as a criticism of the death penalty. While favoring fairer sentencing, they think that the Court was wrong to accept the argument from arbitrariness in the first place. They think that the death penalty can be just even if it is administered in an arbitrary and discriminatory way. For those who hold this position, evidence showing the continued influence of arbitrary and discriminatory factors would have no force because, in their view, it never was legally or morally relevant to the question of whether death is a just punishment.

This rejection of the argument from arbitrariness has been stated forcefully by Ernest van den Haag, a longtime defender of the death penalty. According to van den Haag,

> the abolitionist argument from capriciousness, or discretion, or discrimination, would be more persuasive if it were alleged that those selectively executed are not guilty. But the argument merely maintains that some other guilty but more favored persons, or groups, escape the death penalty. This is hardly sufficient for letting anyone else found guilty escape the penalty. On the contrary, that some guilty persons or groups elude it argues for extending the death penalty to them.[6]

For van den Haag, the only injustice that occurs here is that some people who deserve death are not executed. In his opinion, however, the failure to execute these fortunate people does not show that it is unjust to execute others who are no more deserving of death but are simply less fortunate.

From van den Haag's point of view, the justice of punishments is entirely a matter of individual desert. As he writes:

Justice requires punishing the guilty—as many of the guilty as possible, even if only some can be punished—and sparing the innocent—as many of the innocent as possible, even if not all are spared. It would surely be wrong to treat everybody with equal injustice in preference to meting out justice at least to some....[If] the death penalty is morally just, *however discriminatorily applied to only some of the guilty*, it does remain just *in each case* in which it is applied.[7]

According to van den Haag, then, the justice of individual punishments depends on individual guilt alone and not on whether punishments are equally distributed among the class of guilty people.

Van den Haag's argument is important because it threatens to undermine the moral basis of the *Furman* decision. It dismisses as irrelevant the abolitionist argument that the death penalty is unjust because its use in the United States has been inextricably bound up with patterns of racial discrimination. Even if we find this history abhorrent, we may yet think that van den Haag's argument is plausible. Its plausibility derives from the fact that we believe that it is often legitimate to punish or reward people, even though we know that others who are equally deserving will not be punished or rewarded. Here are two cases where common sense appears to support van den Haag's view about the requirements of justice.

A. A driver is caught speeding, ticketed, and required to pay a fine. Although we know that the percentage of speeders who are actually punished is extremely small, we would probably regard it as a joke if the driver protested that he was being treated unjustly or if someone argued that no one should be fined for speeding unless all speeders were fined.

B. A person performs a heroic act and receives a substantial reward, in addition to the respect and admiration of his fellow citizens. Because he deserves the reward, we think it just that he receive it, even though many equally heroic persons are not treated similarly. That most heroes are unsung is no reason to avoid rewarding this particular heroic individual.

Both of these cases appear to support van den Haag's view that we should do justice in individual cases whenever we can and that our failure to treat people as they deserve in all cases provides no reason to withhold deserved punishment or reward from particular individuals. If this is correct, then we must give up the argument from arbitrariness and accept van den Haag's view that "unequal justice is justice still."

Arbitrary Decisions About Who Deserves What

In order to evaluate this objection to the argument from arbitrariness, we need to look at the original argument more closely. What a closer look reveals is that there is in fact more than one problem of arbitrariness. Van den Haag fails to take note of this, and for this reason, his discussion leaves untouched many of the central issues raised by the argument.

We need to distinguish two different arguments, which I will call the argument from arbitrary judgment and the argument from arbitrary imposition. In making this distinction, I do not mean to contrast two stages in the actual legal process. Rather, the contrast is meant to help us focus on two different grounds for the claim that the death penalty is unjust because arbitrary.

Van den Haag assumes that judges and juries can and do make nonarbitrary judgments about what people deserve and that the problem of arbitrariness arises only in the imposition of punishments. For him, the arbitrariness arises when we try to determine who among those who deserve to die will actually be executed. This is what I want to call the argument from arbitrary imposition. It assumes that we know who deserves to die, and it objects to the fact that only some of those who deserve to die are executed. This version of the argument is expressed by Justice Stewart in the passage which I quoted earlier, and it is this argument which van den Haag addresses.

In doing so, however, he completely neglects the argument from arbitrary judgment. According to this argument, the determination of *who* deserves to die is itself arbitrary. It is not simply that arbitrary factors determine who among the deserving will be condemned to die. Rather, the problem is that the judgment concerning who deserves to die is itself a product of arbitrary factors. In other words, van den Haag assumes that we know who the deserving are, but this is just the assumption that the second form of the argument challenges.

Charles Black is clearly drawing our attention to the problem of arbitrary judgment when he writes that

> the official choices—by prosecutors, judges, juries, and governors—that divide those who are to die from those who are to live are on the whole not made, and cannot be made, under standards that are consistently meaningful and clear, but . . . they are often made, and in the foreseeable future will continue to be made, under no standards at all or under pseudo-standards without discoverable meaning.[8]

If Black is correct, judgments about who deserves a particular punishment are arbitrary because the law does not contain meaningful standards for distinguishing those who deserve death from those who deserve imprisonment. Given this lack of standards, factors that should have no influence will in fact be the primary bases of decision.

This important argument is completely neglected by van den Haag. In order to defend the death penalty against this criticism, he would have to show that our laws contain adequate criteria for deciding whether people deserve death or imprisonment and that judges and juries have made judgments of desert in a nonarbitrary way. Van den Haag makes no effort to do this. He simply assumes that the legal system does a good job of distinguishing those who deserve to die from those who do not. This, however, is just what the argument from arbitrary judgment challenges.

Van den Haag's assumption may gain plausibility from his tendency to oversimplify the kinds of judgments that need to be made. In contrast with Black, who stresses the complexity of the law of homicide and the many steps in the legal process leading toward punishment, van den Haag is content with the abstract maxim that "justice requires punishing the guilty . . . and sparing the innocent." This maxim makes it look as if officials and jurors are faced with the simple choice of dividing people into two neat categories, the guilty and the innocent. And if we think of these as *factual* rather than *legal* categories, it makes it look as if the only judgment that they must make is whether one person did or did not kill another.

In fact, of course, the judgments that must be made are much more complicated than this. To be guilty of a murder that merits the death penalty is not the same as having killed another person. While the basic factual judgment that one person has caused the death of another is itself not always easy to make, the legal judgments involved are more complex still. Of those who kill, some may have committed no crime at all if their action is judged to be justifiable homicide. For those guilty of some form of homicide, we need to decide how to classify their act within the degrees of homicide. What did the killer intend to do? Was he under duress? Was he provoked by the victim? Did he act with malice? Had the act been planned or was it spontaneous? These are among the factual issues that arise when juries try to determine the legal status of the action. Beyond these are legal questions. Was the act murder or manslaughter? And if it was murder, was it first or second degree murder? And if it was first degree murder, did any of the mitigating or aggravating circumstances characterize the act? These are the sorts of issues that actually confront prosecutors, juries, and judges, and they go well beyond the more familiar "whodunit" types of questions.[9]

If prosecutors, juries, and judges do not have clear criteria by which to sort out these issues or if the criteria can be neglected in practice, then judgments about who deserves to face death rather than imprisonment will be arbitrary. This would undermine van den Haag's optimistic assumption that it is only those who genuinely deserve execution who are sentenced to die.

In stressing the complexities of the judgments involved, I have tried to show why it is plausible to believe that the resulting judgments could well be influenced by arbitrary factors. Further, I assume that if we are not confident that the death penalty is imposed on those who truly deserve it, then we would reject the punishment as unjust. This is the moral force of the argument from arbitrary judgment. Even if those who deserve to die ought to be executed, we ought not to allow the state to execute them if the procedures adopted by the state are unlikely to separate the deserving from the undeserving in a rational and just manner. History supports the view that the death penalty has been imposed on those who are less favored for reasons which have nothing to do with their crimes. The judgment that they deserved to die has often been the result of prejudice, and their executions were unjust for this reason.[10]

Is the System Still Arbitrary?

One may wonder, however, whether this sort of arbitrary judgment is still occurring in the administration of the death penalty. Is there any evidence for the continued presence of this form of arbitrariness? Didn't the Supreme Court's Gregg decision show that this sort of arbitrariness is no longer a problem?

To decide whether the problem of arbitrariness remains, one could either examine the new laws themselves to see whether the criteria for selecting those who deserve death are clear and adequate, or one could study the actual legal process and its results to see what factors play a role in leading to actual sentences. Both types of investigations have been carried out, and the case for continuing arbitrariness and discrimination is quite strong. Since my primary purpose here is to show that the existence of arbitrariness is morally relevant to our assessment of the death penalty, I will mention only a few points that indicate that the system remains flawed by arbitrariness. Others have made the case for the persistence of arbitrariness with force and in great detail.[11]

In his book *Capital Punishment: The Inevitability of Caprice and Mistake*, Charles Black shows how unclear are the lists of mitigating and aggravating circumstances which are supposed to guide juries in their sentencing decisions. His purely legal analysis is strongly supported by evidence about the actual workings of the system. In a study of sentencing under the new post-*Furman* laws, William Bowers and Glen Pierce found strong evidence of continued and systematic racial discrimination in the process leading to a sentence of death. I will mention just a few items from their study.

Under the new laws, as they were applied between 1972 and 1977, the highest probability of a death sentence was found to occur in those cases where the killer was black and the victim white. The lowest probability of execution was found where the victim was black and the killer white. This same pattern emerged in a study by William Bowers and Glen Pierce of sentencing in Florida, Georgia, Texas, and Ohio. In Ohio and Florida during this period, there were 127 cases of whites killing blacks, and not one of these murderers was sentenced to death. At the same time, blacks who killed whites in these states had about a 25 percent chance of receiving a death sentence.[12]

The following chart, taken from the Bowers and Pierce study, shows the relationship between the races of victims and killers and the probability of a death sentence as this was exhibited in Ohio between 1974 and 1977.

Racial Grouping	Total	Death Sentences	Death Sentence Probability
Black kills white	173	44	.254
White kills white	803	37	.046
Black kills black	1170	20	.017
White kills black	47	0	.000

These findings strongly suggest that judgments about the seriousness of crimes and the amount of blameworthiness attaching to criminals are strongly influenced by deep-seated racial prejudices. It appears that judges and juries regard the killing of a white by a black as a more serious crime than the killing of a black by a white. Thus, they judge that blacks killing whites deserve more severe punishments than whites killing blacks. Given the bluntness of our ordinary moral judgments and the deep roots of racial prejudice in our society, it is perhaps not surprising that these results occur. But it is clear that no law which embodied these criteria, grading crimes by the race of victims and offenders, would be constitutional. Yet the administration of our laws reveals the de facto operation of just these discriminatory criteria.

Whatever role the criteria for assessing murders play, they do not effectively prevent the operation of discriminatory influences, and so they fail to eliminate the arbitrariness which the *Furman* ruling condemned. Rather than genuinely guiding judgments, the lists of mitigating and aggravating circumstances seem only to provide the language by which juries can justify judgments made on other grounds. This view is further supported by other data in the Bowers and Pierce study. If one compares the Florida and Georgia death penalty statutes, the following difference emerges. In Georgia, the law lists ten aggravating circumstances. If a jury finds *one* of these circumstances characterizing a particular murder, it can recommend death, and the judge *must* accept their recommendation. In Florida, eight aggravating circumstances are listed, and the jury must determine that aggravating circumstances outweigh mitigating ones. On this basis, they can recommend death, but the judge need not accept their judgment.

As a result of these differences, Florida juries must find more aggravating circumstances to support a recommendation of death than do Georgia juries. It is plausible to suppose that murders in Florida and Georgia do not themselves differ in systematic ways. If jury judgments about aggravating circumstances differ systematically, that would suggest that judgments about whether the defendant ought to be executed are made independently of the criteria and then fitted to the criteria in order to provide a legal rationalization for the decision. In particular, while it is implausible to suppose that murders committed in Florida are objectively worse than those committed in Georgia, we might expect to find that juries discover more aggravating circumstances in Florida so as to justify their independent conviction that a particular individual deserves to die.

This is just what Bowers and Pierce found. While juries in Georgia found 46 percent of the murders they considered to be especially vile or heinous, Florida juries found these features in 89 percent of the murders they judged. Likewise, while Georgia juries found the factor of "risk to others" in only 1 percent of the cases facing them, Florida juries found that 28 percent of their murders involved a risk to the lives of others beyond the victim. Similar results are found in all but one of the categories compared, further confirming the judgment that "guided discretion" remains a rather unguided and arbitrary process. The criteria function more as rationalizations of sentencing decisions than as determinants of them.

Finally, while there are many stages in the legal process leading to an execution, the Supreme Court's decision in Gregg focused only on the question of whether juries were provided with adequate guidelines in capital cases. It is important to recall, however, that important decisions are made by prosecutors, judges, governors, and clemency boards as well. The case of prosecutors is especially important and instructive. Prosecutors must decide what charges to file, whether to try to convict a person of manslaughter or murder and whether to press for the death penalty. In making these decisions, they often consider how good a chance they have of winning a case. This does not seem unreasonable, but it is easy to see how this could perpetuate and play upon racial and other prejudices. The black defendant or killer of a white victim may be more likely to be charged with first degree murder in the first place because the prosecutor expects to find a jury that is less sympathetic to these defendants.[13] In many cases, those who are already disadvantaged in society have a greater chance of being charged with more serious crimes, while others more fortunate never face a life or death judgment from a jury because their killing has been classified as manslaughter by the prosecutor. The process is unjustly discriminatory and is arbitrary as well because the judgment is not based on a notion of what the defendant deserves. It is based on a calculation of success or failure in court, which is itself influenced by factors which ought to play no role in the legal process.

Conclusions

In this chapter, we have seen that the system of capital punishment does not operate so as to execute people only on the basis of what they deserve. Other arbitrary factors play a significant role in determining who is to die for killing another human being. In *Furman v. Georgia*, the Supreme Court recognized that an injustice could occur even in cases where a person who is condemned to die actually deserves that punishment. I have tried to explain the moral basis for considering this an injustice.

I have also considered the objection that arbitrariness is irrelevant because justice requires only that those who are punished deserve it. How others are treated is irrelevant. In replying to this objection, I noted the importance of distinguishing two forms of the argument from arbitrariness— the argument from arbitrary judgment and the argument from arbitrary imposition. What I have tried to show is that van den Haag neglects the argument from arbitrary judgment and assumes that all those who are sentenced to die deserve this treatment. This optimistic assumption is unfounded, however, and I have cited some of the evidence that death sentences remain arbitrary and discriminatory in spite of the guided discretion system which the Supreme Court approved in *Gregg v. Georgia* and has upheld in subsequent decisions.

I should note that although much of the arbitrariness I have discussed arises from patterns of racial prejudice in the United States, this argument is not only relevant to the death penalty in our society. There is nothing unique about the situation in which societies contain both favored and unfavored groups. The groups may be identified by race, religion, class, political orientation, or other features. Wherever these divisions exist, arbitrariness and discrimination will be obstacles to the just administration of the law.

| 5 |

The Problem of
Unjust Deserts

IN CONSIDERING THE INFLUENCE of arbitrary factors on the death penalty, I have argued that we cannot rely on the legal system to make correct judgments about who deserves to die. Arbitrariness and discrimination cause jurors and officials to make two different kinds of errors. On the one hand, they are led to decide that a person deserves to die when in fact he does not. In these cases, racial or other prejudice produces sentences which are harsher than deserved. This is one half of the arbitrary judgment problem, and I trust that death penalty advocates would agree that the death penalty system is seriously unjust if people are given more severe sentences than they deserve because they are victims of prejudice.

The second half of the arbitrary judgment problem is that members of favored racial, social, or economic groups may be treated more leniently than they deserve because of their favored status. In this case, arbitrary influences cause jurors to decide that a person does not deserve death when in fact he does. If we imagine only the second of these influences operating, then we approach the problem of arbitrary imposition.

The Problem of Arbitrary Imposition

In considering whether the arbitrary imposition argument shows that the death penalty is unjust, we need to imagine the following situation: everyone who is condemned to die in fact deserves it, but some who deserve to die are given lesser punishments for no good reason. This is different from the real world because in the imaginary example, no one is judged more harshly than he deserves, while in the real world arbitrary factors lead to undeserved severity as well as undeserved leniency. Nonetheless, by considering the imaginary case, we can see why even those who deserve a particular punishment may be treated unjustly when it is imposed on them.

Returning to my earlier example, suppose that red-headed people are the only ones who are ever sentenced to die. Red heads who deserve lesser punishments get lesser punishments, while people who do not have red hair get lesser punishments no matter what they deserve. All red heads who deserve to die are executed. This is the problem of arbitrary imposition. Everyone who is executed deserves to die, but not all who deserve to die are executed. Our question is whether these punishments are unjust.

One might think that the only injustice here is that some people are treated too leniently and that no injustice is done to those who get what they deserve. This is the view defended by van den Haag, and, as I noted earlier, our acceptance of the fact that only some speeders are fined and only some heroes rewarded seems to support this conclusion.

I want to show that this view is mistaken and that the justice of individual rewards and punishments *is* affected by how other people are treated. I will begin by describing two cases in which people get what they deserve but which nonetheless strike us as cases of unjust treatment. Like the earlier cases of the speeders and the heroes, these examples have nothing to do with the death penalty, but they are instructive because they help us to discover features of our general principles of justice. When these principles are better understood, we can then apply them to the death penalty itself.

Each of the following cases is quite parallel to the earlier examples of the punished speeder and the rewarded hero. Yet, somehow things seem amiss in these instances.

A. I tell the students in my class that anyone who plagiarizes will fail the course. Three students plagiarize papers, but I give only one a failing grade. The other two, in describing their motivation, win my sympathy, and I give them passing grades.

B. At my child's birthday party, I offer a prize to the child who can solve a particular problem. Three children, including my own, solve the puzzle. I cannot reward them all, so I give the prize to my own child.

In both of these cases, as in the earlier ones, only some of those who deserve a reward or punishment receive it. Unlike the earlier cases, however, the actions taken here do not appear to be just. Why is this?

I think that what strikes us as unfair in these cases is that the reasons for picking out those who are rewarded or punished are irrelevant to the decision about what they deserve. If I have announced that I will fail students who plagiarize, then it is unjust for me to pass students whom I know to be guilty of plagiarism but with whom I sympathize. Whether or not I am sympathetic to them is irrelevant, and in passing the students with whom I sympathize, I am treating unjustly the student with whom I do not sympathize. Rather than acting simply on the basis of what people deserve, I am acting on the basis of desert and degree of sympathy, and this seems unfair. Likewise, in the case of the prize, I appear to be preferring my own child in giving out the reward, even though I announced that receipt of the prize would depend only on success in solving the puzzle. Even though my child deserves the prize, an injustice is being done in my giving it.

Matters are made worse when the kinds of actions I have described are performed in some systematic way. Suppose, for example, that the very same thing happens at my child's birthday party the following year. Again there are too few prizes, and again, I give the prize to my child. When criticized for favoritism, I protest that it was better that someone get the prize and that I just happened to give it to my child. We would reject this explanation and would see a clear preference operating, a preference which is illegitimate in this context. Likewise, suppose that over a period of years, I am regularly more lenient toward plagiarizers who are attractive females, wealthy students, or sports heroes. What in one instance may be an excusable lapse from strict justice becomes a more serious injustice when these systematic patterns emerge. They make it clear that the real determinants of reward and punishment are not the stated rules and criteria.

Obviously, this is the very point that abolitionists have made about the imposition of the death penalty in our society. Justice Douglas expressed it in his *Furman* opinion, writing that

A law that stated that anyone making more than $50,000 would be exempt from the death penalty would plainly fall, as would a law that in terms said that blacks, those who never went beyond the fifth grade in school, those who make less than $3,000 a year, or those who were unpopular or unstable should be the only people executed. A law which in the overall reaches the same result in practice has no more sanctity than a law which in terms provides the same.[1]

The point holds and the injustice remains even if the departures from the stated laws and criteria are unintentional. This is clear in both the birthday and the plagiarism cases. Moreover, the injustice is compounded when one persists in one's policies even after the effects of systematic discrimination are made evident.

In his discussion of justice, van den Haag asserts that it would be "wrong to treat everybody with equal injustice in preference to meting out justice at least to some." The examples I have discussed suggest otherwise. The plagiarist who fails and the child who receives the prize are not being treated justly, even though they get what they deserve. It would have been better—because more just—to have failed no one than to have failed the single student, just as it would have been better to have given the prize to no one rather than to my child alone.

Doing justice turns out to be more complicated than we often suppose. While it is natural to think that we do justice whenever we give people what they deserve, this common sense belief is mistaken. In many cases, whether one is treated justly or not depends not only on what one deserves but on how other people are treated as well.[2]

The implications for the death penalty are clear. If death is arbitrarily imposed on only some who deserve it, while others equally deserving are treated more leniently, then those who are executed are treated unjustly, even if they deserved to die.

The Inevitability of Arbitrariness

One may feel the force of these arguments and still be troubled by the conclusion. After all, isn't it inevitable that arbitrary factors will play a role in determining who is punished and to what degree? For example, some people who commit crimes are caught because they are unlucky. A chance passerby sees the criminal escaping. Or a particular criminal may not be as skillful or intelligent as others. That does not mean that he is more deserving of punishment. Nonetheless, it makes it more likely that he will be punished, while other smarter, more skilled or just luckier people violate the law and escape any penalty at all. Certainly, we do not think that none of the guilty should be punished simply because some escape.

This objection makes an important point, but it does not undermine the conclusion that the justice of individual punishments is affected by how other people are treated and that individual desert is not sufficient for establishing justice. What the objection shows is that we must distinguish between different kinds of arbitrary factors. The influence of some arbitrary factors is both inevitable and tolerable, while the influence of others is morally unacceptable.

Those factors which are essentially matters of luck or which lie beyond the limits of our control and responsibility can simply be ignored. While we cannot identify all those who commit crimes, it does not follow from this that punishing those that we do detect and convict is unjust. To require that we successfully detect and convict all criminals is to demand that we be omniscient and omnipotent. Moreover, and this is a point we will return to, we must consider the alternatives available to us, and we would be much worse off if we did away with punishment altogether. So, we accept our limitations and do the best we can in catching the guilty.

There are other factors quite separate from questions of guilt, innocence, and degree of desert that also cause some of the guilty not to be punished and that we find acceptable for very different kinds of reasons. Earlier, I noted that we allow some who are guilty to go free because they have been tried and acquitted. Even if new evidence of their guilt emerges later, we do not retry them. Our reason in this case is that we think that a legal system that prohibits double jeopardy is better than one that permits it. As citizens, we want protection against crime, but we also want protection against government harassment and abuse. The institutions of government can be used as effectively against innocent citizens as they can against criminals. For this reason, we are willing to exempt some of those who deserve punishment in order to support an array of legal safeguards whose function is to protect citizens by limiting government power. While this results in equally deserving people being treated differently, this difference is justified by our need for a legal system that does not itself threaten our rights and well-being.

Matters are quite different, however, when the arbitrary factors arise because of prejudicial and discriminatory attitudes that favor some people and work to the disadvantage of others. Our laws do not permit punishing people for racial, religious, or economic status. We are committed to the ideal of "equal justice under law," so when discriminatory attitudes operate as they have in the case of the death penalty, this must be condemned. To accept it would be to accept a legal system that was fundamentally and essentially unjust.

We need, then, to differentiate among the various forms of arbitrariness. Some of them do undermine just treatment, while others are morally acceptable. The importance of making this distinction can be made clearer by returning to the example of the unticketed speeders. In general, we do not think that a ticketed speeder can justifiably complain that he is being treated unjustly on the ground that other equally guilty speeders do not receive tickets. We accept this degree of arbitrariness in the system because we know that it is impossible to have perfect enforcement of speed limits. We know that not all who speed can be detected, and we accept this.

Nonetheless, while our sense of justice is not offended by partial enforcement of speeding laws, it does not follow that every means of determining which speeders to ticket would be equally just. A policy of ticketing every tenth speeding car would be less good than a policy of ticketing those which are traveling at extremely high speeds. Yet, either of these would be superior to a policy of ticketing only those speeding drivers with beards and long hair or only those whose cars bear bumper stickers expressing unpopular political views. In the latter cases, the ability to enforce traffic laws is being used as a tool to punish people for their personal appearance or for their political views. These policies involve unjust abuse of power by officials.

Most of us are not offended by selective enforcement of speed limits because we know that total enforcement is impossible, and we probably think that police officers give out tickets either to those driving most dangerously or in a somewhat random fashion. While a purely random policy may not seem entirely fair, it is much to be preferred to various kinds of unjust discrimination based on irrelevant features of the drivers. Finally, it is important, too, that the punishments in these cases are rather mild and that we believe that some social good (safer roads) is attained through these enforcement efforts. They keep a lid on highway speeds, even though the lid is not as tight as the stated legal limit.

Contrast these features with the case of the death penalty. There is strong evidence that the disparate treatment of people is not merely random. Nor is it the case that only the most dangerous are executed. Instead, systematic discrimination plays an important role in determining who is sentenced to die and who receives lesser punishments. Finally, unlike the traffic case, these punishments are extremely severe, and there is no evidence that they serve any useful purpose, since long prison sentences seem to be as effective in their deterrent power. In the speeding case, we would feel quite differently if the punishment were extremely severe and served no useful purpose. Yet, this is precisely the case with the death penalty.

As I have emphasized before, the death penalty is a system, not merely a way of dealing with individuals. Whether the death penalty is just or unjust depends largely on its systematic features, how it operates as a whole. To see whether it is just or unjust, we must look not only at whether those executed deserve to die but also at whether others equally deserving are equally treated.

Living with Imperfect Justice

Supporters of the death penalty might concede that I have shown that there is some injustice in executing murderers who deserve to die and yet continue to deny that the death penalty must be abolished. While admitting the force of the argument from arbitrary imposition, they might reply that some arbitrariness (even of the unjustified forms) is inevitable in any legal system and that we simply cannot expect our institutions to be perfect.

This is exactly the defense of the death penalty that van den Haag raises. He writes:

> The Constitution, though it enjoins us to minimize capriciousness, does not enjoin a standard of unattainable perfec-

tion or exclude penalties because that standard has not been attained....I see no more merit in the attempt to persuade the courts to let all capital-crime defendants go free of capital punishment because some have wrongly escaped it than I see in an attempt to persuade the courts to let all burglars go because some have wrongly escaped imprisonment.[3]

It is an important feature of this objection that it could be voiced even by those who concede the injustice of arbitrarily imposed death sentences. Lamentably, they might say, we must simply live with this injustice. Why? Because arbitrariness pervades the criminal justice system, and if we were to abolish the death penalty on grounds of arbitrariness, we would likewise have to abolish all criminal punishment.

At this point, the argument from arbitrariness can be turned against death penalty opponents. It might be argued that if arbitrariness provides a sufficient reason for abolishing the death penalty, then it provides a sufficient reason for abolishing all punishments. Death penalty opponents, then, must either (a) argue for abolishing all criminal punishments—which is absurd, or (b) concede that the arbitrariness of the system does not provide a compelling reason for abolishing the death penalty— which would mean giving up their view.

Is there a way out of this dilemma for death penalty opponents?

I believe that there is. Opponents of the death penalty can continue to support other punishments, even though their administration is affected by arbitrary factors, while maintaining their opposition to the death penalty. This is not to say that anyone should be content with arbitrariness and discrimination significantly affecting the imposition of any serious punishments. Quite apart from the death penalty, there are profound injustices that need to be combatted.[4] Nonetheless, the problem of arbitrariness arises against the death penalty with special force. There are two primary reasons for this.

First, death is a much more severe punishment than imprisonment. This is almost universally acknowledged by people on both sides of the death penalty debate. It is recognized by the law as well, since special procedures are required in capital cases. Death obliterates the person, depriving him or her of life and thereby, among other things, depriving him or her of any further rights of legal redress or appeal. For the person who is executed, discoveries of new facts or new interpretations of the law cannot provide new opportunities for appeal or review. In this connection, it is worth recalling that hundreds of people were executed and are now dead because they were tried and sentenced under the pre-*Furman* laws, which, in Justice Douglas' words, allowed the "uncontrolled discretion of judges and juries."

Because of the finality and the extreme severity of the death penalty, we need to be more scrupulous in applying it as punishment than is necessary with any other punishment. Moreover, if we find injustices in its application, we should accept them only if the death penalty is absolutely necessary. Yet, as we have seen in our discussion of deterrence, there is no reason to believe that the death penalty saves lives. Thus, while the general system of punishment is necessary for maintaining social order, the death penalty is not necessary to secure our safety.

Even people who are distressed by the injustice that pervades the criminal justice system admit that we must live with it, doing the best we can to make it fairer and more equitable. Most of us believe that if we were to abolish all punishments, we would produce a Hobbesian state of social chaos in which many more innocent people would be killed and injured and in which no one would be secure. That is why death penalty opponents can support the punishment system generally. It is necessary for human rights and human well-being. The same cannot be said, however, for the death penalty, which seems to play no protective role at all. The argument from arbitrariness has a special force when applied to death as a punishment that it lacks when turned on the punishment system in general. For this reason, death penalty opponents can consistently support the one while condemning the other.

Conclusions

In this chapter, I have tried to show how it could be unjust to execute someone, even if we assume that he deserves to die. This is possible because the justice of a punishment is crucially affected by factors other than what a person deserves. Even people who get their just deserts may be punished unjustly.

One reason why this is usually not evident to us is that our ordinary moral thinking is conducted on an individual rather than an institutional level. We tend to think that individual justice—giving people what they deserve—provides an adequate model for the design of institutions. If someone deserves to die, then it seems natural that we should empower the state to execute that person.

In supporting the death penalty, however, one supports a system in which some people are authorized to decide who deserves to die. That decision, however, may be flawed, influenced by factors that have nothing to do with desert, and dependent on factors we would not approve or support as conditions of punishment. In attempting to institutionalize the moral judgment that some murderers deserve to die, we have created a system that makes no moral or legal sense, a system that has the added flaw of exacerbating the liabilities and disadvantages that already fall on some citizens. These are genuine problems of justice. They provide powerful reasons for rejecting the death penalty, even if one is convinced that those who murder deserve to die.

| 6 |

Do Murderers
Deserve to Die?

In the last two chapters, we have seen that even if we assume that murderers deserve to die, there are many good reasons against imposing the death penalty. For people who believe that murderers deserve to die but who accept the arguments of the last two chapters, the fact that we cannot justly execute murderers is lamentable. Ideally, from their point of view, it would be best if we could execute murderers because that is what they deserve. Unfortunately, we cannot rely on our institutions to distinguish those who deserve death from those who do not. Therefore, we cannot rely on them to execute all and only those who deserve to die. Ideally, we would give people what they deserve, but we are forced by our sense of equal justice to restrain ourselves.

These strong feelings of dissatisfaction arise from the deep conviction that death is the uniquely appropriate punishment for at least some murderers. Nothing that I have said so far shows that this conviction is mistaken, but I believe that it is mistaken and will now try to explain why.

In criticizing the view that murderers deserve to die, I do not mean to suggest that murderers ought not to be punished. Nor do I wish to oppose severe punishments for murderers. Rather, I want to argue that it is wrong to think that what murderers deserve dictates the appropriate punishment for them, and it is wrong to think that death is the only appropriate punishment for murder. It is the links between murder, deserving, and death that I shall try to sever.

Deciding What People Deserve

Discussions of what murderers deserve are likely to reach an impasse very quickly. There are firm convictions on each side, but few arguments and no apparent agreement about how to decide whether or not murderers deserve to die.

Faced with this sort of breakdown, the best thing to do is to shift our focus and try to see how we determine what people deserve in other circumstances. After all, we make judgments about what people deserve in many kinds of situations, and if we see how we know what is deserved in other cases, we may be able to return to the controversy about what murderers deserve with some general principles to apply.

How then do we tell what someone deserves?

In many situations, this is not difficult at all. Our judgments are made in the context of an activity, and there are familiar rules which govern what people engaged in that activity deserve. In races, for example, the first to cross the finish line deserves the prize, while in lotteries the deserving person is the one whose ticket is drawn. In a classroom, the student who answers all questions correctly deserves a good grade. In each of these settings, there is a prior understanding of the criteria of desert. The criteria may be written down or informally understood, but everyone knows how to apply them and thus how to judge what people deserve. This does not mean that such judgments are always easy to make. Two runners may be so close that it is hard to tell which one crossed the line first, but even in this controversial case, there is no disagreement about the criteria that determine desert.

Many legal cases fit this pattern and are distinguished only by the tendency toward formality and explicitness. Given what the law says, we have no trouble determining that a speeder deserves a fine, that a delinquent taxpayer deserves to pay a penalty plus interest, or that a consumer deserves a refund if he bought a faulty product that carried a money-back guarantee.

In all of these cases, what a person deserves is defined by the explicit rules or informal understandings involved in particular activities or situations. Whenever desert is determined in this way, I will speak of it as *institutional* desert.

Because institutional desert judgments are familiar to us from many areas of life and because they can often be made relatively easily, it would be very helpful if we could rely on them as a model for determining whether murderers deserve to die. Unfortunately—and for a number of important reasons— we cannot do this.

One reason why the institutional desert model provides no help here is that institutional desert is not the same as *moral* desert, and the judgment that death penalty advocates are making is that murderers deserve to die in a moral sense. The moral and institutional senses of desert, however, are quite different. We can see that moral desert and institutional desert are different by looking again at some of the cases I mentioned. When we say that a person deserves something in a moral sense, we are making an appraisal of that person, yet when we say of the person with the winning lottery ticket that she deserves the prize, we are in no way appraising her character or moral worth. Likewise, if the winner of the race owes her speed to a wonder drug while the runner-up trained long and hard, we may well think that the loser morally deserved to win, even if we acknowledge that, in the institutional sense, the winner deserves the prize. So, the kind of judgment involved in institutional contexts is different from the type of moral judgment that death penalty advocates are making about murderers.

There is another reason why institutional desert judgments are no help to those who believe that murderers deserve to die. While death penalty advocates believe that murderers deserve to die in some stable and deep sense, institutional desert is a shallow, variable, and purely conventional notion. We can change what a person institutionally deserves simply by changing the rules. If we wanted to test for patience rather than speed, we could make the last runner to cross the finish line the winner. Or, we could call the person whose ticket is not drawn (after all the rest are) the winner of the lottery prize. There is nothing natural about being fastest or first drawn that requires us to reward them. If these examples seem odd, recall that in golf it is the low score which wins, while in bowling, the high score brings victory. Thus, there is nothing at all fixed about institutional desert. We can change it at will. Yet, death penalty advocates do not believe that what murderers deserve depends on existing legal rules or could be changed simply by holding a vote or issuing a proclamation.

Death penalty advocates cannot appeal to any sense of institutional desert to support their judgment that murderers morally deserve to die. While it is true that in states with death penalty statutes, murderers who are tried, convicted, and sentenced to death *legally* deserve to die, this is not a fact to which death penalty advocates can appeal. This comes out most clearly if we consider what would happen if the death penalty were legally abolished. If death penalty supporters were relying on the notion of institutional legal desert, then they would have to give up their view that murderers deserve to die because the legal criteria of desert would have changed. But it is clear that death penalty advocates would not do this. Instead, they would oppose the law and would favor changing it so as to make it conform to their independent moral judgment that murderers deserve to die. Where the law allows executions, then death penalty advocates appeal to what murderers morally deserve to show that the existing laws are appropriate. Similarly, when the law does not allow executions, they appeal to moral desert to show why the law should be changed. The idea of moral desert which they appeal to in both cases is different from the purely legal, institutional form of desert which we find in the law and many other contexts.[1]

The key point here is that while institutional desert is a familiar notion, there are no institutions to which we can appeal in determining what murderers morally deserve. If death penalty advocates want to show that murderers deserve to die, they cannot look to existing social, political, or legal institutions to justify their judgment. They must provide us with some other way of determining what people deserve. Moreover, it may turn out that once we leave behind the assistance of institutional frameworks, judgments of desert may become more difficult both to make and to justify.

An Eye for an Eye?

Suppose we leave behind institutional frameworks, then, and try to determine what people deserve from a strictly moral point of view. How shall we proceed?

The most usual suggestion is that we look at a person's actions because what someone deserves would appear to depend on what he or she does. A person's actions, it seems, provide not only a basis for a moral appraisal of the person but also a guide to how he should be treated. According to the *lex talionis* or principle of "an eye for an eye," we ought to treat people as they have treated others. What people deserve as recipients of rewards or punishments is determined by what they do as agents.

This is a powerful and attractive view, one that appears to be backed not only by moral common sense but also by tradition and philosophical thought. The most famous statement of philosophical support for this view comes from Immanuel Kant, who linked it directly with an argument for the death penalty. Discussing the problem of punishment, Kant writes,

> What kind and what degree of punishment does legal justice adopt as its principle and standard? None other than the principle of equality...the principle of not treating one side more favorably than the other. Accordingly, any undeserved evil that you inflict on someone else among the people is one that you do to yourself. If you vilify, you vilify yourself; if you steal from him, you steal from yourself; if you kill him, you kill yourself. Only the law of retribution (*jus talionis*) can determine exactly the kind and degree of punishment.[2]

Kant's view is attractive for a number of reasons. First, it accords with our belief that what a person deserves is related to what he does. Second, it appeals to a moral standard and does not seem to rely on any particular legal or political institutions. Third, it seems to provides a measure of appropriate punishment that can be used as a guide to creating laws and instituting punishments. It tells us that the punishment is to be identical with the crime. Whatever the criminal did to the victim is to be done in turn to the criminal.

In spite of the attractions of Kant's view, it is deeply flawed. When we see why, it will be clear that the whole "eye for an eye" perspective must be rejected.

Problems with the Equal Punishment Principle

There are two main problems with this view. First, appearances to the contrary, it does not actually provide a measure of moral desert. Second, it does not provide an adequate criterion for determining appropriate levels of punishment.

Let us begin with the second criticism, the claim that Kant's view fails to tell us how much punishment is appropriate for particular crimes. We can see this, first, by noting that for certain crimes, Kant's view recommends punishments that are not morally acceptable. Applied strictly, it would require that we rape rapists, torture torturers, and burn arsonists whose acts have led to deaths. In general, where a particular crime involves barbaric and inhuman treatment, Kant's principle tells us to act barbarically and inhumanly in return. So, in some cases, the principle generates unacceptable answers to the question of what constitutes appropriate punishment.

This is not its only defect. In many other cases, the principle tells us nothing at all about how to punish. While Kant thought it obvious how to apply his principle in the case of murder, his principle cannot serve as a general rule because it does not tell us how to punish many crimes. Using the Kantian version or the more common "eye for an eye" standard, what would we decide to do to embezzlers, spies, drunken drivers, airline hijackers, drug users, prostitutes, air polluters, or persons who practice medicine without a license? If one reflects on this question, it becomes clear that there is simply no answer to it. We could not in fact design a system of punishment simply on the basis of the "eye for an eye" principle.

In order to justify using the "eye for an eye" principle to answer our question about murder and the death penalty, we would first have to show that it worked for a whole range of cases, giving acceptable answers to questions about amounts of punishment. Then, having established it as a satisfactory general principle, we could apply it to the case of murder. It turns out, however, that when we try to apply the principle generally, we find that it either gives wrong answers or no answers at all. Indeed, I suspect that the principle of "an eye for an eye" is no longer even a principle. Instead, it is simply a metaphorical disguise for expressing belief in the death penalty. People who cite it do not take it seriously. They do not believe in a kidnapping for a kidnapping, a theft for a theft, and so on. Perhaps "an eye for an eye" once was a genuine principle, but now it is merely a slogan. Therefore, it gives us no guidance in deciding whether murderers deserve to die.

In reply to these objections, one might defend the principle by saying that it does not require that punishments be strictly identical with crimes. Rather, it requires only that a punishment produce an amount of suffering in the criminal which is equal to the amount suffered by the victim. Thus, we don't have to hijack airplanes belonging to airline hijackers, spy on spies, etc. We simply have to reproduce in them the harm done to others.

Unfortunately, this reply really does not solve the problem. It provides no answer to the first objection, since it would still require us to behave barbarically in our treatment of those who are guilty of barbaric crimes. Even if we do not reproduce their actions exactly, any action which caused equal suffering would itself be barbaric. Second, in trying to produce equal amounts of suffering, we run into many problems. Just how much suffering is produced by an airline hijacker or a spy? And how do we apply this principle to prostitutes or drug users, who may not produce any suffering at all? We have rough ideas about how serious various crimes are, but this may not correlate with any clear sense of just how much harm is done.

Furthermore, the same problem arises in determining how much suffering a particular punishment would produce for a particular criminal. People vary in their tolerance of pain and in the amount of unhappiness that a fine or a jail sentence would cause them. Recluses will be less disturbed by banishment than extroverts. Nature lovers will suffer more in prison than people who are indifferent to natural beauty. A literal application of the principle would require that we tailor punishments to individual sensitivities, yet this is at best impractical. To a large extent, the legal system must work with standardized and rather crude estimates of the negative impact that punishments have on people.

The move from calling for a punishment that is identical to the crime to favoring one that is equal in the harm done is no help to us or to the defense of the principle. "An eye for an eye" tells us neither what people deserve nor how we should treat them when they have done wrong.

Proportional Retributivism

The view we have been considering can be called "equality retributivism," since it proposes that we repay criminals with punishments equal to their crimes. In the light of problems like those I have cited, some people have proposed a variation on this view, calling not for equal punishments but rather for punishments which are *proportional* to the crime. In defending such a view as a guide for setting criminal punishments, Andrew von Hirsch writes:

> If one asks how severely a wrongdoer deserves to be punished, a familiar principle comes to mind: Severity of punishment should be commensurate with the seriousness of the wrong. Only grave wrongs merit severe penalties; minor misdeeds deserve lenient punishments. Disproportionate penalties are undeserved—severe sanctions for minor wrongs or vice versa. This principle has variously been called a principle of "proportionality" or "just deserts"; we prefer to call it commensurate deserts.[3]

Like Kant, von Hirsch makes the punishment which a person deserves depend on that person's actions, but he departs from Kant in substituting proportionality for equality as the criterion for setting the amount of punishment.

In implementing a punishment system based on the proportionality view, one would first make a list of crimes, ranking them in order of seriousness. At one end would be quite trivial offenses like parking meter violations, while very serious crimes such as murder would occupy the other. In between, other crimes would be ranked according to their relative gravity. Then a corresponding scale of punishments would be constructed, and the two would be correlated. Punishments would be proportionate to crimes so long as we could say that the more serious the crime was, the higher on the punishment scale was the punishment administered.

This system does not have the defects of equality retributivism. It does not require that we treat those guilty of barbaric crimes barbarically. This is because we can set the upper limit of the punishment scale so as to exclude truly barbaric punishments. Second, unlike the equality principle, the proportionality view is genuinely general, providing a way of handling all crimes. Finally, it does justice to our ordinary belief that certain punishments are unjust because they are too severe or too lenient for the crime committed.

The proportionality principle does, I think, play a legitimate role in our thinking about punishments. Nonetheless, it is no help to death penalty advocates, because it does not require that murderers be executed. All that it requires is that if murder is the most serious crime, then murder should be punished by the most severe punishment on the scale. The principle does not tell us what this punishment should be, however, and it is quite compatible with the view that the most severe punishment should be a long prison term.

This failure of the theory to provide a basis for supporting the death penalty reveals an important gap in proportional retributivism. It shows that while the theory is general in scope, it does not yield any *specific* recommendations regarding punishment. It tells us, for example, that armed robbery should be punished more severely than embezzling and less severely than murder, but it does not tell us how much to punish any of these. This weakness is, in effect, conceded by von Hirsch, who admits that if we want to implement the "commensurate deserts" principle, we must supplement it with information about what level of punishment is needed to deter crimes.[4] In a later discussion of how to "anchor" the punishment system, he deals with this problem in more depth, but the factors he cites as relevant to making specific judgments (such as available prison space) have nothing to do with what people deserve. He also seems to suggest that a range of punishments may be appropriate for a particular crime. This runs counter to the death penalty supporter's sense that death alone is appropriate for some murderers.[5]

Neither of these retributive views, then, provides support for the death penalty. The equality principle fails because it is not in general true that the appropriate punishment for a crime is to do to the criminal what he has done to others. In some cases this is immoral, while in others it is impossible. The proportionality principle may be correct, but by itself it cannot determine specific punishments for specific crimes. Because of its flexibility and open-endedness, it is compatible with a great range of different punishments for murder.[6]

A More Serious Objection

So far, in looking at these versions of retributivism, I have tried to show that they do not help us to determine the appropriate punishment for specific crimes. That is, they do not really tell us what sort of treatment is deserved by people who have acted in certain ways.

There is a more serious defect of both versions of the theory, however. Neither one succeeds in basing punishment on what a person morally deserves. Why is this? Because both theories focus solely on the action that a person has performed, and this action is not the proper basis for determining moral desert. We cannot tell what a person deserves simply by examining what he has done.

While it may sound odd to say that a person's degree of moral desert is not determined by his actions, the point is actually a matter of common sense morality. We can see this by considering the following examples, all of which are cases of rescuing a drowning person.

1. A and B have robbed a bank, but B has hidden the money from A. A finds B at the beach and sees that he is drowning. A drags B from the water, revives him, finds out the location of the money, and then shoots him, leaving him for dead. The shot, however, is not fatal. A has saved B's life.
2. C recognizes D, a wealthy businessman, at the beach. Later, she sees D struggling in the water and, hoping to get a reward, she saves him. C would not have saved D if she had not thought that a reward was likely.
3. E is drowning at the beach and is spotted by F, a poor swimmer. F leaps into the water and, at great risk to her own life, manages to save E.
4. G is drowning at the beach but is spotted by Superman, who rescues him effortlessly.

In each of these cases, the very same act occurs. One person saves another from drowning. Yet, if we attempt to assess what each rescuer morally deserves, we will arrive at very different answers for each case. This is because judgments of desert are moral judgments about people and not just about their actions or how they should be treated. Our moral judgments about A, C, F, and Superman in the examples above are quite different, in spite of the similarity of their actions. From a moral point of view, we would not rate A as being praiseworthy at all because he had no concern for B's well-being and in fact wished him dead. C, the rescuer motivated by the prospect of a reward, wished D no harm but is also less praiseworthy because her act was not motivated by genuine concern for D's well-being. Finally, while F, the poor swimmer, and Superman both acted from benevolent motives, F is more deserving of praise because of the greater risk which she took and the greater difficulties she faced in accomplishing the rescue.

What these cases make clear is that there is no direct connection between what a person does and his or her degree of moral desert. To make judgments of moral desert, we need to know about a person's intentions, motivations, and circumstances, not just about the action and its result. Since both Kant and von Hirsch base their judgments concerning appropriate punishments simply on the act that has been committed, they do not succeed in basing their recommended punishments on what a person morally deserves, for what a person deserves depends on factors which they do not consider.

It is quite ironic that Kant overlooks this and provides an exclusively act-oriented account of assessing people in his discussion of punishment. In other writings, Kant insists that the fact that an action is harmful or helpful does not by itself tell us how to assess the moral value of the agent's performing it.[7] He lays great stress on the significance of motivation, claiming that the moral value of actions depends *entirely* on whether they are done from a moral motive.

"Payback" Retributivism

With this criticism in mind, it is instructive to look back at the passage from Kant about the need to execute murderers. What is striking about the passage is that Kant does not talk about desert at all. He does not say that a person deserves to die because he has killed and therefore that he ought to be executed. Rather, he says that a person should be executed simply because he has killed.

The lack of any reference to moral desert in this passage is more than just a linguistic oversight by Kant. It reflects the existence of a form of retributivism that is related to but different from the view that I have been discussing. I have assumed that the central retributivist ideal is that people ought to get what they deserve. But there is another view of retribution, according to which justice is done when a person is paid back for what he does. In this famous passage, Kant expresses the "payback" version of retributivism rather than a form of the view that focuses on moral desert. Why this is I do not know, but in any case, Kant is not alone in thinking that retribution has been achieved when a person has been treated as he has treated others.

Although retribution is often cited as a goal of the criminal law, this "payback" conception is weak and unattractive. First, it provides no justification for punishment. We want to know why it is morally permissible to punish someone who has committed a crime, and the answer of the "payback" retributivist is simply that it is permissible to pay people back for their deeds by doing to them what they have done to others. This reply begs the question by offering no independent reason for punishing. By contrast, one who justifies punishment by saying that the person being punished deserves this treatment appears to be offering a substantive, independent reason for punishing, making this view much more attractive than the "payback" conception. He is pointing to some feature of the person which makes the punishment appropriate.

Second, the "payback" retributivist defines the actions people have committed by reference to the *results* of those actions. If we consider this view, however, it is easy to generate conclusions that the retributivist himself would find unacceptable. When people who believe in "an eye for an eye" say that those who kill must be killed in turn, this cannot possibly be their final word on the matter. If it were, then they would be committed to the view that those who kill accidentally must be killed. More absurdly, they would have to hold that whenever the death penalty is imposed, the executioner of the murderer would in turn have to be killed because he has killed, as would the executioner of the executioner and so on.

These absurd conclusions can, of course, be avoided by describing actions in more sophisticated ways. Doing this makes it possible to deny that accidental and intentional killings are the same. It allows us to distinguish the intentional killing done by the original murderer from the intentional killing performed by the executioner. Having done this, we can call one of these acts murder, a second accidental homicide, and the third a legal execution. Furthermore, we then say that it is only murderers— and not those who commit accidental homicide or perform legal executions—who should be paid back for their deeds. Once we do this, however, we have moved away from the "payback" version of retributivism and its simple focus on the results of actions. In distinguishing these various killings, we have been forced to look at motives, intentions, and circumstances and not just to consider actions and results. To do this is to leave behind "payback" retributivism and to return to the more complex "giving people what they deserve" version of the theory. Indeed, this is the most plausible version of the theory. Retributivism without desert is simply too crude a view to be plausible.

Any reasonable principle, then, will recognize that not all killings are murders and hence that not all who kill deserve to die. This is, in fact, the view of common sense morality, which sanctions some types of killing (for example, killing in self-defense) and thus allows that one who kills may even be morally blameless. Furthermore, even among those killings that are illegitimate and that we want to classify as murder, not all are equally reprehensible. This is reflected in the Supreme Court's judgment that mandatory death sentences for murder are unconstitutional.[8] Though the Court often speaks the language of retribution, its decisions depart from the simplicity of "payback" retributivism.

Conclusions

In this chapter, I have examined some of the arguments that might be used to defend the view that murderers deserve to die. I have tried to show why these arguments fail. The traditional versions of retributivism do not justify death as a specific punishment for murder. Moreover, in their usual forms, they omit factors that are essential to determining what a person deserves. Paradoxically, one cannot tell what a person deserves simply by knowing what he has done. In particular, it is not enough to know that someone has killed someone else or even that he has done so unjustifiably. The examples of the various rescuers show that we must consider more than a person's deeds to determine what he or she deserves.

At this point, one might suggest that I have been unfair to advocates of the death penalty. After all, the standard homicide laws require that we take account of motives, intentions, and other features of a criminal's actions and character that are relevant to desert. If we consider these factors, perhaps we can distinguish between those killers who deserve to die and those who do not.

Death penalty advocates might charge that I have only shown that not all who kill deserve to die, but if we define murder properly, we may be able to show that at least some of those who murder deserve to die. Let us see whether this proposal can be carried out.

| 7 |

Deserving to Die

IN DEFENDING THE VIEW that murderers deserve to die, death penalty supporters tend to focus on the quality of the act that a murderer has performed. To make their argument complete, however, they need to tell us how moral desert is measured or determined. If we have no criteria for judging moral desert, we cannot tell what murderers deserve.

In chapter 6, we saw that death penalty supporters cannot appeal to institutional criteria of desert to justify their view that murderers deserve to die. They cannot do this because institutional criteria of desert are purely conventional, highly variable, and generally have nothing to do with appraisals of moral desert. Likewise, they cannot appeal to a crude "eye for an eye" approach, which focuses only on the act that a person has performed. As we saw in the case of the various rescuers, the same act can be correlated with different degrees of moral desert. In order to judge what a person deserves, we need to look beyond the act and its results and examine other factors, such as motives and intentions. Let us see, then, whether it is possible to formulate criteria of desert that are more subtle, more complex, and sufficiently strong to support the judgment that murderers deserve to die.

A More Complex View of Moral Desert

One might think that by delaying the discussion of criteria of desert, which include motivation, intention, and other relevant factors, I have been unfair to proponents of the death penalty. No one would deny that these factors are relevant, and the law explicitly includes them in the definition of murder and other crimes. The legal doctrine of *mens rea* makes the presence of certain intentions necessary even for a crime to have occurred. These factors enter into the definitions of murder, manslaughter, and other criminal acts. In addition, variations in motive and intention are frequently used to determine the severity of the punishment. Most death penalty supporters probably believe that death is the appropriate punishment only for those who kill intentionally and whose acts display an especially high degree of callousness, indifference, or brutality.

These judgments suggest a kind of retributive theory that is more enlightened and attractive than the one expressed by the "eye for an eye" principle. It will be worth seeing how we might develop such a view of moral desert in a systematic way. Then we can examine its implications for the death penalty.

A plausible version of this view can be sketched along the following lines.[1] If a person is correctly judged to be negatively deserving or morally blameworthy, then he must have violated some moral rule. The violation must have been done knowingly and voluntarily, for in most cases, we do not consider someone morally blameworthy if his behavior was accidental or involuntary (unless he was reckless or negligent in some way). Moreover, he must have acted from a motive that we regard as bad, for even if someone causes harm, we may not think him morally blameworthy if he "meant well."

In addition to guiding our judgments about when a person is morally blameworthy, this approach will also guide us in deciding the degree of personal blameworthiness. Because moral rules vary in importance, violating some moral rules will make one more blameworthy than violating others. It is worse to kill someone than to tell a lie, and therefore murderers are more blameworthy than liars. Likewise, some breaches of a moral rule are more serious than others. It is worse for me to steal your life savings than your weekly paycheck, although both actions violate the same rule. In addition, there are degrees of voluntariness, and we recognize that duress or provocation may make people less blameworthy for their deeds. Finally, there are degrees of badness in motives and intentions. We would usually rank an act done from sadistic cruelty as worse than one done in anger or from jealousy.

These kinds of criteria could presumably be worked out in much greater detail. Even with this short sketch, however, we can see why not all killings are murders, why murder is so grave a crime, and why some murders are worse than others. First, not all killings are done "knowingly and voluntarily," and in many cases, when these factors are missing, we totally absolve a person of moral responsibility. (Where negligence is a factor, of course, a person may still be blameworthy to some degree.) Murder does always involve a breach of a moral rule—the rule against unjustified killing. The gravity of murder is a function of the fact that the rule against killing is an extremely serious moral rule, more important than prohibitions against lying or breaking promises. Finally, the person's motive or desire must be bad if he is to be fully blameworthy. Whatever one thinks about the morality of euthanasia, it is clear that the "mercy killer" is less reprehensible than the killer for hire because the mercy killer is motivated by a benevolent desire. Moreover, the worse the motive, the more blameworthy is the murderer.

There is much more that needs to be said and done in order to work out a complete scheme that orders types of killings according to their degrees of gravity. Much of the law of homicide has been a continuing attempt to do this, and the intent often (though not always) seems to be a desire to make the law conform to our moral sense of how wrong certain sorts of acts are. Let us assume that this enterprise could be completed and that we would have a full list of categories of killings, one that is sensitive to differences in motive and intention and that ranks types of killings according to their moral gravity. Presumably, defenders of the "murderers deserve to die" thesis would then settle on those acts which appear to be among the worst murders and would claim that people who commit these acts are morally blameworthy to an extremely high degree. Finally, they would conclude that people who are morally blameworthy to this degree deserve to die and ought to be executed.

The Failure of the More Complex View of Desert

This view, though far superior to the simpler theories of desert with which we started, is still unsatisfactory and does not provide real support for the death penalty. There are a number of reasons for this.

First, even if we could construct an adequate scale of personal moral desert, it would not follow from the fact that a person received the maximum negative rating that he deserved to be killed. The view we have been discussing assumes that some form of proportionality retributivism is true and therefore that punishments should be proportional to crimes. Yet, as we saw in discussing von Hirsch's "commensurate deserts" idea, a proportionality system does not require any specific form of punishment for any type of crime. Even after we have ranked crimes according to gravity, there is no necessity in fixing the minimum or maximum levels of punishment at any particular point. The worst murderers (as judged by our complex moral desert scale) would deserve the worst punishments, but the worst punishment in the system need not be death. It could be a "fate worse than death," such as prolonged torture, followed by eventual execution. Or, it could be a less severe punishment, such as life in prison, exile, ten years of hard labor, or a $500 fine. All of these are consistent with the proportionality view, since it does not specify the degree of punishment for crimes. Someone could accept the proportionality view, agree that a particular murderer is extreme in his moral depravity, and still not know what specific punishment is appropriate to this person.

That this is possible reveals an ambiguity in the notion of desert. Words having to do with moral desert sometimes refer to a *quality of a person* ("He is a deserving individual") and sometimes to the *treatment* appropriate to a person ("He got his just deserts"). In speaking of *what* a person deserves, we usually have in mind a particular kind of treatment or response from us, of which punishments and rewards are two types. But in talking about what people morally deserve, we are also making appraisals of them. We attribute some degree of moral desert to them, and that property (degree of moral desert) is the basis for our judgment that they should be treated in a particular way. The hero deserves our praise or a reward because of his heroic nature. The criminal deserves punishment because of his culpability. In this sense, moral desert is a property of a person, not a treatment or response to a person.

To be ill-deserving and to deserve a specific ill are two different matters. Once we see that these are different, then we can see why one can judge a person to be negatively deserving (in the sense of being a morally bad person) without being committed to the view that he deserves some specific treatment. So an opponent of the death penalty could agree that a particular murderer is the worst sort of person and yet disagree that he deserves to die. There is no inconsistency in such a view, and death penalty advocates must show why persons with the maximum degree of negative moral desert ought to be killed rather than treated in some other extreme, negative manner.

So, even if this more complex system of determining desert were adequate, it would still leave open the question of what punishment is appropriate for those who commit the worst sorts of murders. It would not show that death was the only appropriate punishment for such people.

Efforts and Obstacles

We have seen that even if an approach which considers intentions and motives provides an adequate measure of personal moral desert, it still does not justify particular punishments for particular crimes. That is not its only weakness, however. In spite of its superiority over the crude views discussed earlier, this conception of moral desert is itself badly flawed. Like the earlier view, it leaves out factors that are relevant to judgments of moral desert and therefore does not really give us adequate criteria for making personal moral appraisals.

We can see this most easily by considering the actions of the insane, who may intentionally perform wrong actions with malicious motives and still not be morally blameworthy. The same is true of young children. In both cases, we do not regard the people involved as full-fledged moral agents. For this reason, we do not make negative moral judgments of them, in spite of their wrong actions and their bad intentions. This shows that the "actions plus intentions" view is not a complete account of the criteria of moral desert.

We need not focus on children or the insane, however, in order to see the insufficiency of the view we are discussing. We can see it by continuing to think generally about how we appraise people and their degrees of desert. When we judge moral desert, we do not look solely at people's actions, motives, and intentions. We often look at other factors. In particular, we are frequently concerned with the amount of effort required for someone to act or

m acting in a certain way. The importance of this factor
sized by Elizabeth Beardsley in her study of moral
desert. She writes,

> As agents, we are often convinced that acts eliciting a consider-
> able amount of praise from outsiders were somehow for us
> unusually "easy," and in these cases we do not seem to our-
> selves to deserve high praise. Correspondingly (and doubtless
> far more often) we are convinced as agents that certain acts
> eliciting considerable blame from outsiders were for us such
> that acts alternative to them would have been somehow un-
> usually "difficult," and here we feel that we do not deserve
> much blame.[2]

Beardsley's remarks remind us of the importance which effort
often has in our judgments, and they suggest the insufficiency of
desert judgments based only on information about actions and
motives. Even if someone acted badly with bad motives, there
may be other factors that made it especially difficult for that
person to act in any other manner. If we discover this, we may
retract or modify our judgment about the degree to which the
person is negatively deserving.[3]

While Beardsley appeals to judgments about ourselves, we
often have similar feelings about the erroneousness of moral
appraisals of others. Herman Schwartz, commenting on von
Hirsch's "commensurate deserts" principle, raises the issue in
quite concrete form. Registering his dissent from the principle, he
asks rhetorically,

> Can one really say that someone *deserves* to be punished for
> breaking the law, when that person may have been hooked on
> heroin by the time he was a teenager, was confronted with
> racism or other prejudice, grew up in a broken home amid
> violence, filth, and brutality, was forced to go to substandard
> schools, and had no honest way to make a decent living?[4]

Schwartz expresses a familiar and plausible view here. His question suggests that a person brought up in extremely unfortunate
circumstances may not be fully deserving of blame if he fails to
act in a morally appropriate manner. His acts may be wrong, but
he himself is not morally blameworthy or at least not as
blameworthy as he would have been had he benefited from more
fortunate surroundings. This is because his conditions made it

especially difficult or perhaps impossible for him to act otherwise.[5]

The central point here is that a person's degree of moral desert
is determined primarily by considerations of what could reasonably be expected of him. If a person faces such powerful obstacles
to moral behavior that it would require extraordinary amounts of
effort to act well, then, though he acts badly, he is not morally to
blame. Almost anyone in that situation would have acted similarly, and different behavior could not reasonably be expected.
The causes of difficulty need not be environmental. They could be
physical, psychological, or of any sort, but if they make alternative actions extremely difficult or impossible, a person is not
fully blameworthy for his deeds, even if they were wrong acts
triggered by bad motives.

The importance of effort as a central factor in determining
genuine moral desert will be recognized by many people. The
effort-oriented criterion of moral desert is a part of moral common
sense and is reflected in many of our ordinary beliefs. We tend to
think that people who have worked hard are more deserving of
their wealth than people who have inherited money or won
lotteries. We think that one who trains hard deserves to win a race
more than one who just naturally can run very fast. Likewise, in
the rescue examples, the poor swimmer deserves more credit for
rescuing the drowning person than does Superman. She had to
overcome both her fears and the objective difficulties of the rescue, while Superman could perform the rescue effortlessly. We
give people the most moral credit when their good deeds require
them to exert a great deal of effort, and we think that people are
not fully deserving of blame when we judge that the effort required for acting rightly is greater than what could reasonably be
expected of them.

The importance of effort is likewise reflected in the familiar
maxim that we ought not to judge another person unless we know
what it would be like to be "in his shoes." The idea here seems to
be that we cannot legitimately blame someone unless we know
that it was possible for that person to act otherwise than he did
and that we could only know whether this was possible by being
in the other person's shoes, that is, by seeing and feeling things
from his perspective. One need not agree with this view to recognize that it is a common one and that it reflects an awareness in

moral common sense that many of our immediate judgments of people fail to take the difficulties of their situation seriously enough.

What Follows?

What is the upshot of these reflections? What are the implications of the "effort criterion" of moral desert?

The first thing that follows is that making adequate judgments of moral desert is not easy. Matters are difficult enough when we are trying to discern a person's motives and intentions. They become more difficult still when we try to grasp whether someone was in a position to behave in ways other than he did. Some of these difficulties (as well as additional support for the correctness of the effort criterion) are nicely brought out in some insightful remarks by Friederich Hayek. Although Hayek is writing about economic justice rather than criminal justice, his points apply directly to our concern. He thinks that questions about economic justice (that is, about how wealth ought to be distributed) cannot be decided by appealing to what people deserve or merit. Moral desert is not, in his opinion, a proper basis for economic justice because it is too difficult to know just how deserving someone is. In describing what one would have to know in order to determine someone's degree of moral desert, he writes:

> To decide on merit presupposes that we can judge whether people have made such use of their opportunities as they ought to have made and how much effort of will or self-denial this has cost them; it presupposes also that we can distinguish between that part of their achievement which is due to circumstances within their control and that part which is not.[6]

In order to make these kinds of judgments, we would require both substantial biographical and psychological information about individual people and much greater general knowledge of the determinants of human behavior than we have access to.

Second, if this "effort" view of desert is true, then there is no automatic connection between having performed a certain action with certain motives and being praiseworthy or blameworthy to some degree. The same act could be performed by two people with the same intentions, yet one would be morally blameworthy and the other not. Why? Because one's background or psychological makeup made it especially difficult or impossible for him not to act this way, while the other's background made it relatively easy.

The extreme difficulty of making these judgments of moral desert suggests that we should adopt a somewhat skeptical attitude toward them. This skepticism might take several forms. We might conclude that it is impossible for us ever to know just how morally blameworthy a person is. There are simply too many factors and too much information required for a full and reliable assessment. This conclusion is reflected in the familiar idea that only God can really judge a person. The reason for this is that only an omniscient being could know enough about a person to know what he was able to do or refrain from. If this view is true, then we cannot know what people morally deserve and therefore cannot know that someone who murders deserves to die.

This extreme skepticism is not the only possibility. A more moderate view would be that although such judgments are very difficult to make, they are not impossible. With sufficient care, effort, and attention, one could take into account enough of the relevant factors and make reasonable moral appraisals of people. Like all judgments, these could be wrong, but there is no insuperable barrier to making them. Nonetheless, according to this second view, it is not reasonable to expect that our legal institutions will produce such subtle and complex judgments in a rational and unbiased way. Judges, prosecutors, jurors, and other officials who act within the legal system are under many practical constraints and are influenced by many factors that have nothing to do with the moral desert of an accused person. We have already seen the influence of racial prejudice and other arbitrary factors on legal decisions about degrees of guilt. Because of these influences, we cannot count on our legal institutions to make judgments of moral desert in a fair, informed, and rational way. Therefore, even if knowledge about what people morally deserve is theoretically possible, we ought not to expect it to be obtained in the legal context.

There is a third conclusion that is less radical than the extreme skepticism of the first view and that would help explain the arbitrariness of institutional judgments emphasized by the second view. According to this third view, there are no precise amounts of moral desert, and it is therefore impossible to develop a precise scale for measuring desert. When we evaluate people from a moral perspective, our judgments can be correct if we state them in a relatively vague way and make no pretensions to exactness. There is nothing wrong with judgments like "he is a good person," or "she deserves to be treated better." However, if we try to determine degrees of desert as if there were a precise scale of desert, then we go wrong, for there is no precise scale. If two people are guilty of terrible murders, we are mistaken in thinking that if we examine the cases closely enough, we will find that one of them rates a − 99 on the desert scale and the other rates a − 100. Worse yet, we are mistaken if we think that anybody who scores − 100 deserves to die, while those who score − 99 deserve a lesser punishment. The fundamental error is to believe in the precise scale at all.[7]

Once we see that there is no precise scale, then it becomes clearer why prejudice and other irrelevant factors enter into these judgments of desert. They enter in because without an objective guide, people are left to their feelings about the victim and the defendant, and their feelings will flow from their general values, their social attitudes, and their ability to identify with the victim or the murderer. Under the guise of an attempt to determine the precise degree of a defendant's moral culpability, they will simply be measuring their own degree of distaste for him and his actions.

Doesn't Anyone Deserve Anything?

I want to be careful not to be misunderstood, especially since my view is open to a particularly unattractive misinterpretation.

Someone might think that I am arguing that no one is responsible for what he does at all and that we can never say of someone that he deserves good or ill. Neither of these things follows from my view.

I have suggested three possible conclusions about judgments of moral desert. The first was a radically skeptical view, according to which we can never know whether people are genuinely morally deserving. If we think that our judgments about what people morally deserve would all be undermined by the truth of determinism, then we will be sympathetic to this view. For if determinism is true, then all of our actions result from events that could not have been different, and we could not act differently from the way we do.

Even if we accept this radical view, we would have good reasons for *holding* ourselves and others responsible for our actions. These standards would be justified even if it turned out that none of us could behave any differently from the way that we do. The standards would be justified as social mechanisms by which we try to ensure that people will be spared from various forms of pain, injury, and deprivation. The basic justification for holding people responsible is that this practice provides support for important human and social values.[8] This pragmatic, utilitarian justification for holding people responsible is especially appropriate to our discussion, because it is the primary justification for the criminal law and the institution of punishment. As I have argued earlier, the primary purpose of the law is protective. So, even if we cannot guarantee that people are genuinely morally deserving of punishments, we can set up fair institutions that protect people and that are justified by their protective role rather than by the conception of the law as the enforcement arm of morality.

Indeed, the focus on effort and desert brings out an additional aspect of social standards of responsibility. One of the factors that influences the degree to which people can maintain control and act in the face of difficulties is the extent to which others expect them to do so. In a society in which no one was held responsible and all immoral actions were thought to be the product of unavoidable causes, people would accept the fact that they could not maintain self-control and would be more likely to act badly. Where people are expected to act decently, even in the face of provocation, temptation, and other obstacles, they are more likely to retain control of themselves. So there is good reason to maintain standards of responsibility, even if we are skeptical that we can know in particular cases that people are fully responsible.

From this perspective, we do not have to be capable of making pure judgments of moral desert because these do not provide the basis of our system of moral and legal responsibility. We punish and blame not because we are certain that our moral appraisals are true but rather because punishment and blame, like reward and praise, provide important support for human values. The defense of these practices is both moral and pragmatic. The pragmatic aspect stresses the usefulness of holding people responsible, while the moral side stresses the fact that the standards are being used on behalf of important human values.

So, even if we accept the most radical of the views about moral desert that I have suggested, my conclusion would not require that we scrap the criminal law or the notion of legal responsibility for our actions.

Having seen this, it should be clear that neither of the other more limited skeptical views requires us to give up our ideas of moral desert and personal responsibility. We can accept the idea that our legal institutions will measure desert only imperfectly without concluding that people should not be held morally or legally responsible for their actions. Likewise, we can reject the idea of a precise moral desert scale without giving up the practice of making moral desert judgments in our ordinary life.

What my arguments do require is that we reject the view that there is a precise moral desert scale which can be used to show that those who murder with certain motives or in certain circumstances deserve to die. Likewise, it is a mistake to think of the criminal law as an institution for giving people what they morally deserve. The law and the system of punishments may be justified even when we are uncertain what people morally deserve, and given the difficulties of determining degrees of moral desert, this is quite fortunate.

Conclusions

In this chapter, I have tried to show that even when we operate with a conception of desert based on actions plus motives, we cannot support the view that murderers deserve to die. This conception, while more complex than other retributivist views, omits the key factor of effort from its measurement of desert.

Those who believe that murderers deserve to die are caught in a dilemma. They can justify their view only by appealing to crude and unacceptable criteria of moral desert. When they try to appeal to more adequate criteria, the judgment that they want to support finds no basis.

If we are serious about judging what others deserve, we must become involved in questions about people that are so complex that it is either impossible for us to resolve them or impossible for our institutions to handle them in a fair and rational manner. Moreover, the notion that murderers (or at least some subset of them) deserve death and that no other punishment is appropriate—that idea presupposes a precise scale of moral desert that does not exist. There is no such thing as a uniquely appropriate punishment for any particular crime. What punishment is appropriate depends on many complex factors and certainly does not flow readily from a conception of what a person morally deserves.

The claim that murderers should be executed because they deserve to die has occupied our attention for four chapters. My attack on this view has been two pronged. First, I argued that even if it were true that some murderers deserve to die, it would not follow that we ought to authorize the state to execute them. I tried to make clear that there are serious grounds for doubting that the state can impose the death penalty in a uniform and rational way. The record of arbitrary and discriminatory judgments should undermine our confidence that the system picks out those who are truly deserving in a systematic way.

Second, I turned to the moral claim that murderers deserve to die and tried to show that it could not be supported. When we work out a satisfactory account of what is involved in moral desert, it becomes impossible to correlate levels of desert with specific actions, even when motives and intentions are built into the description of the actions. Moreover, even if we can appraise people's level of moral desert, there is no specific punishment or treatment which goes with any level of desert. While we can agree that more severe punishments should be reserved for more serious crimes, nothing more definite or specific is required by the principle that people ought to be treated as they deserve. There is no basis for believing either that murderers deserve to die and or that justice is served only when those who murder are punished by death.

| 8 |

Is the Death Penalty Cruel and Unusual?

THE PHRASE "cruel and unusual punishment" comes from the Eighth Amendment to the United States Constitution. It is a legal expression, the meaning of which has been debated by lawyers, judges, and legal theorists. But it is also an expression with strong moral connotations. Whether we understand it morally or legally, the idea conveyed is that there are barriers that limit the form and extent of punishment. No punishment that goes beyond these barriers is acceptable, even if it appears to be justified on other grounds.

Because the limits set by morality and the limits set by law do not coincide, a person who asks whether the death penalty is cruel and unusual punishment may be asking either a moral or a constitutional question. In keeping with the main focus of this book, I will treat this issue primarily as a moral question. I will draw on various court decisions, but I will appeal to them primarily as sources of moral arguments. There may be some risk of distortion in doing this, but it is outweighed by the light shed on our question.

Inherently Barbaric Punishments

The most natural reading of the ban on cruel and unusual punishments is that it forbids the use of such practices as torture, dismemberment, boiling in oil, burning at the stake and other treatments which cause so much pain as to be barbaric. In times past, many of these treatments were widely accepted, and indeed torture remains a widespread practice in our own day.[1] Nonetheless, there is general agreement that these forms of treatment are grossly immoral.

If one could show that the death penalty was on a par with these barbaric actions, that would provide a powerful reason against it. But it is not clear that one can show this. To many opponents of the death penalty, it seems obvious that it is inherently barbaric. The deliberate killing of a living human being in the most calculating manner, even after that person has ceased to be a threat to society at large, appears to be ghastly and inhuman. For death penalty supporters, however, the punishment is dreadful but appropriate because of what the person himself did. As long as death is not caused in a manner which produces excessive and unnecessary pain, they find executions to be compatible with humanity and civility.

If we understand the question "Is the death penalty cruel and unusual?" to mean "Are executions inherently barbaric?," then I see no way to resolve this dispute. Indeed, thinking about the question in terms of the intrinsic or inherent nature of the act may simply direct us away from the important issues.

It appears, in fact, that whether an act is barbaric or not depends on the context in which the act occurs rather than on its intrinsic features. What counts as torture, for example, depends not just on the physical action performed but on the reasons for doing it. A torturer might saw off a person's leg, causing excruciating pain and leaving him disabled for life. The same act, performed without anesthesia on a person with a gangrenous leg by a 19th-century surgeon, would be an act of healing. We could not tell just by looking at the physical process whether we were witnessing a medical procedure or a torturing session. Both acts might present revolting spectacles, yet that would not show that they are morally equivalent.

The need to consider the context of the act counts against both those who see executions as inherently barbaric and those who do not. A person who thinks that execution by lethal injection is inherently barbaric might well think that a lethal injection would be merciful and humane if administered to a terminal patient who is overwhelmed by pain. In that context, the act does not look barbaric at all. It would be wrong for death penalty supporters, however, to take delight in this and argue that lethal injections are obviously morally acceptable. A lethal injection administered to an innocent person by a murderer is a dreadful act of murder, the very sort of act which death penalty supporters are rightly horrified by. So, the fact that such injections are relatively painless and might be morally acceptable in some settings does not imply that they are morally acceptable in all situations. Likewise, the fact that it may be easier to witness a lethal injection than an electrocution does not mean that it is a morally legitimate form of punishment.

Looking at the inherent qualities of actions alone is a dead end that casts no light on the moral acceptability of death as a punishment. Asking whether an act is morally right is not the same as asking whether we are revolted by its occurrence. If our question does take that form, it is easy to understand why debate about it would lead to stalemate, since we are not all revolted by the same things. In order to tell whether an action is cruel and unusual, we must look elsewhere.

A Broader View

It is easy to think that our idea of a cruel and unusual punishment is exhausted by the notion of what is inherently barbaric. Nonetheless, the Supreme Court has interpreted the idea more broadly, and it is easy to see that our ordinary idea is broader as well. In a number of cases, the Supreme Court has ruled that a punishment can be cruel and unusual if it is disproportionately severe.[2] A punishment that is appropriate for one crime might be cruel and unusual when imposed for another.

To see that the Court's judgment was reasonable, consider the case of a person receiving a five-year prison sentence for a parking meter violation. In many contexts, five years in prison is thought to be a light punishment, but it would be morally outrageous if it were imposed for a minor violation like failing to put money in a parking meter. While there is nothing inherently barbaric about a five-year prison term and nothing the matter with punishing people for parking meter violations, the combination of that punishment for that illegal act is extraordinary. It is wrong to inflict that severe a punishment on someone for such a trivial offense.

Having noted that "cruel and unusual" can mean "disproportionately severe," I will not appeal to this sense of the expression in arguing against the death penalty. For many people, death is precisely proportionate to murder. The point that I want to make here is simply that a punishment may be cruel and unusual without being inherently barbaric. The case of disproportionately severe punishments is instructive because it is relatively uncontroversial and establishes that there is a wider sense of "cruel and unusual" than one might think. It shows that punishments need not be obviously similar to torture in order to make them excessively cruel.

Once we see this, it is easier to appreciate the force of the Court's judgment in *Furman v. Georgia*. As we have already seen, the Court decided in that case that a punishment could be cruel and unusual even if it was neither inherently barbaric nor disproportionately severe. What the Court found to be cruel and unusual in that case was that an extremely severe punishment was being imposed in an arbitrary and capricious manner. When a punishment is as severe as death, it is cruel and unusual to impose it (rather than some lesser punishment) for reasons which have nothing to do with the crime a person committed. We would not find it acceptable to use a lottery to determine which of those people convicted of murder should be executed. Nor would we write our laws so as to make the degree of a punishment depend on the race of the victim or the offender. Yet, in effect, the death penalty was being administered in accord with these unacceptable rules.

That the death penalty was cruel and unusual in this sense could not be known simply by witnessing an execution or even by examining the trial records in a particular case to determine whether the punishment was proportionate to the crime. One would have to look at an even broader context, the pattern of sentences that emerges within a large number of cases. Only this sort of investigation would reveal the freakishness and the discrimination which were found to determine whether a person would live or die.

I have already defended the central arguments from the *Furman* case, arguing that punishments imposed in these conditions are unjust. I think that the argument from *Furman* remains a strong one and does establish both the immorality and the unconstitutionality of the death penalty, even as it is practiced today. There is no need for me to say more about this interpretation of the "cruel and unusual" clause.

I do not want to rest with this interpretation, however, because I think that the concept of cruel and unusual punishments is richer than has been indicated so far. I would like to bring out some of this additional richness and to show how it provides additional grounds for rejecting the death penalty.

Cruelty and Excess

In many cases, we permit actions that cause pain and suffering because we think they are necessary for some valuable end. Medical treatments, parental punishments of children, and public criticism of political leaders are some examples of activities that are justified in spite of the pain they cause. None of these need be cruel in any way, and engaging in these acts need not indicate any degree of callousness or insensitivity on the part of the agent.

In each of these cases, however, it is important that there be no way of achieving the good result without the pain. If the same result could be achieved without suffering, then it would be cruel not to choose a less painful means of achieving one's goal. If a physician can administer an anesthetic during a medical procedure and if the anesthetic will relieve the patient's pain without creating other dangers or interfering with the effectiveness of the treatment, then it would be cruel for the physician not to choose the less painful means. Likewise, if a parent can teach a child a lesson by talking to her rather than spanking the child or depriving him or her of some enjoyment, then the appropriate action is to talk to the child. Or, if the same effect could be achieved with a lesser punishment and the parent chooses a more severe punishment anyway, this would also constitute cruel behavior. In each of these cases, an action becomes cruel when there are less painful alternatives to it that are equally effective means of achieving someone's legitimate goals.

The same point applies to criminal punishments. I have already argued that the state has a legitimate right to impose punishments in order to protect its citizens, but this right is not unlimited. Indeed, it is especially important that this right be severely constrained because the kinds of actions done as punishment are actions which are typically immoral and which need special justification. The executioner kills as surely as the murderer. The warden and guards in a prison confine a person against his will in the same way that a kidnapper does. The official who collects a fine takes a person's money against that person's wishes in the same way that a thief does. These acts are all examples of things that are generally immoral to do. If they are justified, what justifies them is the necessity of performing them to achieve some extremely worthwhile end. They may be performed only to the extent that they contribute to this end. If they do not contribute, they become acts of cruelty.

So, having the right to inflict harm under certain circumstances does not mean that one has unlimited permission to do so. Whatever harm one inflicts must be directly related to the ends that justify the practice. Punishing beyond the amount that is necessary for these ends is immoral.

This argument was made by some of the justices in the *Furman* decision. Justice Brennan, for example, cited as one of the four conditions involved in determining whether a punishment is cruel and unusual that "there is no reason to believe that it serves any penal purpose more effectively than some less severe punishment."[3] Justice White developed the point further, arguing that

> the [death] penalty has not been considered cruel and unusual in the constitutional sense because it was thought justified by the social ends it was deemed to serve. At the moment that it ceases realistically to further these purposes, however, the emerging question is whether its imposition in such circumstances would violate the Eighth Amendment. It is my view that it would, for its imposition would then be the pointless and needless extinction of life with only marginal contributions to any discernible social or public purposes. A penalty with such negligible returns to the State would be patently excessive and cruel and unusual punishment violative of the Eighth Amendment.[4]

White clearly links excess with cruelty in this passage and forcefully makes the point that whether a punishment is cruel is determined in part by whether it is necessary for achieving an important social goal. Even a distasteful punishment may be justified if social goals are served by it more effectively than other punishments, but when a punishment ceases to be necessary, then it is excessive and hence cruel.

This argument confirms a point I made earlier about the moral significance of the deterrence argument. For, according to White, the death penalty would not be excessive and cruel if it were a substantially better deterrent of murders than imprisonment. It is excessive because it is not known to be more effective in protecting the lives of citizens. If it could be shown that executions were better deterrents than prison sentences, then the death penalty would not be cruel in this sense. It might still be cruel because it was imposed in an arbitrary and discriminatory manner, but it could not be rejected as cruel because excessive. As things stand, however, the death penalty is cruel in both of these senses, since the evidence we have both shows that it is imposed arbitrarily and fails to show that it is necessary for the defense of people's lives.

Here again, then, the discussion of the constitutional status of the death penalty provides us with an additional moral insight into why it is wrong. Even if the argument from excess were rejected as a basis for constitutional interpretation, it would remain as a powerful moral objection to the death penalty.[5]

Excess and Retribution

Death penalty supporters might agree that lesser punishments deter as well as executions and therefore that the death penalty is excessive for deterrent purposes. They might nonetheless object to this argument, claiming that it falsely assumes that deterrence is the only function of punishment and overlooks the fact that punishment serves a retributive function. Even if the death penalty exceeds the severity necessary for deterring murders, it does not, in their view, exceed what is necessary for retribution. Indeed, according to them, it is the only punishment which is adequately retributive. Imprisonment is insufficient for this purpose.

This objection brings us back to some of the issues I considered in discussing whether murderers deserve to die. In the light of that discussion, we can try to interpret what is meant by saying that death is not excessive from a retributive point of view and, more strongly, that the additional severity of the death penalty is necessary to carry out the retributive function of the law.

On what grounds might one hold that death is necessary for

retribution? Someone might believe that murderers morally deserve to die and thus that only death gives them what they deserve. We have seen, however, that this view requires too crude a conception of moral desert. Given the variety of motives and intentions that lie behind killings, as well as the differences in the amount of effort required for people to control their actions, we cannot say that everyone who kills is maximally blameworthy in a moral sense. Moreover, we have seen that even if someone can be shown to be "maximally blameworthy," it does not follow that death or any other specific treatment of them is required. All that is morally required is that the response be negative and not trivial. Therefore, we cannot say that death is the only appropriate retribution in all of these cases.

Someone might argue that death alone is appropriate because death alone treats the criminal as he has treated his victim. This claim is trivially true, but it does not show that death is required or even permissible. It relies on the suppressed premise that we ought to inflict on criminals the same treatment that they inflicted on their victims. This premise, however, is simply the "eye for an eye" principle once again. We have seen earlier that this principle is unacceptable because it would require us to respond barbarically to those guilty of barbaric crimes. This is especially relevant to our current focus, since it would require cruel and unusual punishments for cruel and unusual crimes. In addition, I have argued that this is not a general principle at all, since we cannot find equivalents for most crimes and hence cannot use this as a guideline in determining what is retributively appropriate.

A third interpretation of the claim that only death is appropriate from a retributive point of view would be that only death is proportionate to the crime. Yet, we have seen earlier that proportionality is a relative notion. What it requires is that more serious crimes be punished more severely than less serious crimes. In addition, it expresses the idea that the punishment for a serious crime ought not to be trivial. It ought not to convey the idea that the crime was insignificant. Part of the concern being voiced by those who talk about the victim is that we not trivialize the loss of the victim's life by imposing minimal punishments.

I do not wish to reject this third sense of retribution. It is worth noting, however, that retribution in this sense is not entirely separate from the deterrent function. We want to convey a message about the degree of seriousness attaching to particular acts. This message will not be conveyed if those who do these acts are treated too leniently, so it is important that punishments be severe enough to convey this message.

All these points can be made in support of the ideal of proportional punishments, but they do nothing to show that the death penalty is justified. What they show is that the punishment of murder must be severe. No one doubts that long-term imprisonment is a severe punishment, however. To confine someone for twenty-five years, thirty years, or a lifetime is not to be lenient, and it does not convey any sense that murder is a trivial crime. These sentences are quite adequate to fulfill the retributive functions of punishment. Even from a retributive point of view, then, death is unnecessarily severe and therefore cruel.

It is worth recalling a point from *Furman* here, the fact that only a small number of those who murder are sentenced to die. Though many favor the execution of murderers as an abstract matter, prosecutors, judges, and juries do not in fact sentence most murderers to death. On a case-by-case basis, they seem to find reasons not to do this, and they seem to find retribution satisfied by lesser punishments. Moreover, as we have seen, when they do choose death, it is not because the crimes are worse and demand greater retribution. The crimes of those sentenced to die are generally undistinguishable from the crimes of those sentenced to lesser punishments.[6] Whatever general pronouncements people make, the demand for death as retribution is not consistently made or followed by the criminal justice system. Lesser punishments are generally accepted as sufficient.

The Limits of State Power

Death is a punishment of extraordinary severity. This is not to say that it is the worst possible punishment. We can imagine forms of torture that are worse, treatments that would make living a curse. But this does not take away from the extremity of death as a punishment. To punish by death is to obliterate the person punished.

That death is a dreadful punishment is agreed to by both sides to this debate. If death penalty supporters did not agree, they would not view murder with such horror, and they would be less likely to attribute such power to the threat of death in deterring murders.

It is an irony of contemporary politics that those who call themselves conservatives and speak the language of limited governmental power tend to favor the death penalty. Yet if one is truly concerned about limiting the power of government to direct or control the lives of citizens, then one will be wary of granting to government officials the power to make life and death decisions. Governments must have this power to some degree if they are to carry out their protective functions. Governments must have the power to go to war against foreign enemies, just as they must have the power to use force against threats from their own citizens. But a true conservative will be stingy in granting these powers to government officials. The right to send people to their deaths will be granted only in that minimal set of areas where it is absolutely necessary for the protection of society.

Contemporary conservatives have left these concerns behind, though they still appeal to slogans which express some of them. It is libertarians and philosophical liberals who have best voiced the arguments against unlimited government. Conservatives have become spokesmen for what I shall call the moralistic state, while liberals and libertarians have defended the restricted state.[7] In its more extreme form, the moralistic state aims for the highest good for society and seeks to insure the highest virtue in its members. Its policies are motivated by religious or other ideals, and its advocates believe that in pursuit of the highest good, governments may direct citizens to find proper values and to pursue the path of righteousness. The moralistic state uses the law to impose a moral order, forbidding actions which are sinful and seeking to give criminals what they deserve.

Advocates of the restricted state see government as much more limited in its aims. Government is essentially a protective device, a set of institutions whose primary purpose is to protect us from violence and other forces which would make our pursuit of the good life impossible. But the restricted state will not tell us what the good life is or seek to impose a moral order on us. The restricted state deals with us as citizens, not as whole persons. This means that we have the freedom to be foolish, unhealthy, and even sinful, provided that we do not threaten the well-being of others. On this view, the state is but one of many associations to which people belong. People are citizens, but their citizenship is not the whole of their lives. Therefore, the state ought not to deal with every aspect of our selves but should only deal with us in our role as citizens.[8]

Citizens are required to obey the laws, and the state may rightfully punish a citizen for violating the law. Punishments may be severe, but they ought always to be limited by the original protective purpose of the state—to provide protection that enables us to live our lives and to pursue our own conceptions of the good life. The essential purpose of punishment on this view is to protect society from violations of the law. It is not to make sure that the wicked suffer. That is a moralistic conception.

The state has a right to punish us if we fail in our duty as citizens, but it can punish us only as citizens. In imposing death as a punishment, the state goes beyond this right. To imprison someone is to take away his civil liberties, his ability to go freely among other members of society. To imprison someone for life will limit his actions and pursuits to a very extreme extent, but it will leave him with something, a part of his life which is not determined or controlled by the state.

Death as a punishment obliterates the person and not just the citizen. When the state punishes by death, it takes away something over which it ought not to have power. The state plays God, making the kind of judgment that God is thought to make of a person in his totality. This kind of total judgment is not one that officials should presume to make. Nor should the state be empowered to inflict the total punishment, the punishment that destroys a person in his entirety.

The right to take the lives of citizens is not something that should be turned over to officials in a casual way. From the point of view of morality, we want justifiable killings to be kept to a minimum, and such authorizations tend to be interpreted too broadly. From the point of view of history, we can see that even the best governments have often been casual in spending the lives of their citizens for ill-considered or immoral purposes. Those who respect human life will be wary about granting others the right and the power to destroy it.

From the perspective of the restricted state ideal, the death penalty is cruel and unusual because it goes beyond the bound-

aries of legitimate state power. It treats people as if it had a claim
to the totality of their lives, rather than limiting its actions to
those that are necessary to the core functions of government. This
is not to say that governments ought never to be authorized to act
in ways which cause people's deaths, but unless there are the
most compelling reasons for doing so, such actions will go beyond the rightful limits of state power.

Conclusions

In this chapter, I have tried to show that the death penalty is
cruel and unusual in a moral sense. While I believe that it violates
the Constitution as well, I will leave it to others to make that
argument.[9] Most of us confront the death penalty as a subject of
moral reflection. Even if the death penalty is legally or constitu-
tionally permissible, that is no guarantee of its morality in any
case. That important moral arguments are often raised in Supreme Court opinions shows that there are overlaps between
morality and the law. Nonetheless, "immoral" and "unconstitutional" are not the same. Slavery, remember, was permitted by the
Constitution and upheld by the Supreme Court. It was nonetheless immoral.

The key points I have tried to make here are that we need not
equate cruel and unusual punishments with those that are inherently barbaric or those that are disproportionately severe. Rather,
punishments can be cruel and unusual if they are imposed
freakishly or for the wrong reasons or if they are more severe than
is necessary for carrying out legitimate state functions. On all of
these criteria, the death penalty is a cruel and unusual punishment.

Finally, I introduced a contrast between the moralistic and the
restricted conception of the state, and I argued that the death
penalty is inconsistent with the restricted conception. This last
argument raises numerous questions of general political philosophy. I offer it more for the general perspective it provides than as a
powerful debating point. Even if it fails to convince, the other
arguments in the chapter provide more concrete and less con-
testable reasons for regarding the death penalty as cruel and
unusual.

|9|

Vengeance and Vigilantism

THE DESIRE FOR VENGEANCE is the desire that someone suffer because of the harm that he has done to another. It is related to the desire for justice, but it is not the same. One can want vengeance even in cases where justice does not demand that anyone be punished. Indeed, one can want revenge even when nothing wrong has been done, as when a criminal might seek revenge against witnesses who had testified against him.

Appeals to vengeance may be relevant to the death penalty in two ways. First, it could be argued that the imposition of the death penalty by the state is legitimate because it is justified by the need for vengeance. Second, it could be argued that even if the state cannot or ought not to execute murderers, the desire for vengeance would justify an individual who seeks to kill a murderer.

We need to begin by describing vengeance a bit more fully. A person who seeks vengeance desires to inflict harm or suffering on another person. What distinguishes the desire for revenge from other desires to injure is that it is a response to a previous harmful act. It is a desire to retaliate for some ill deed. Typically, we think of the person motivated by vengeance as experiencing a great hatred of someone and a strong desire to harm that person. Finally, we often think of there being a special satisfaction which is felt when the person who has done wrong is made to suffer. The original act has been avenged, and the avenger feels better because of this.

In some contexts, the idea of vengeance is simply an alternative expression for the idea of retributive justice. To seek revenge is to want a wrongdoer to get what he deserves, what he "has coming to him." Often this is expressed in terms of the "eye for an eye" principle or the proportionality theory. If the appeal to vengeance is simply another way of presenting these conceptions of justice, then we need not discuss it further, since we have already seen that these theories are flawed and do not justify the death penalty.

In other contexts, it is clear that the ideas of vengeance and of justice are not equivalent, and we need to see whether the appeal to vengeance can provide an independent basis for the death penalty. While the desire for vengeance may not be as intellectually respectable an emotion as the desire for justice, it is too important to neglect.

The Argument from Vengeance

We can best frame the argument from vengeance in the following way. Suppose that people generally have an intense hatred of murderers, that they have a strong desire to see murderers executed, and that they feel great satisfaction when murderers are executed. Finally, suppose that no other punishment gives them the same degree of satisfaction. According to the argument from vengeance, if these conditions exist, then it is legitimate for the state to execute murderers.

As it stands, this argument clearly fails to justify the death penalty. We can see this by substituting some other word for "murderers" in the argument. Suppose that people had an intense hatred of basketball players, felt a strong desire to see them executed, and experienced great satisfaction when this occurred. Surely this would not justify the death penalty for playing basketball. Yet, it is just these emotions that are thought to justify executions in the case of murderers.

One may think that this attempt to undermine the argument from vengeance is absurd. There is all the difference in the world between executing murderers and executing basketball players. I agree, but remember that we are considering the idea that murderers should be executed in order to satisfy the desire for vengeance. If the desire for vengeance is a sufficient reason for executing murderers, then it is a sufficient reason for executing basketball players. If we are tempted to accept the argument as it applies to murderers, that must be because there are additional reasons that make the execution of murderers morally plausible. The most natural reason to appeal to is the idea that murderers deserve to die or that executions are just retribution for murder.

This, however, is an appeal to justice and not an argument from vengeance. It shifts the argument to another basis, rather than reenforcing the basis that vengeance was supposed to supply.

What my admittedly ludicrous example is intended to reveal is that the intense hatred, the desire for harm, and the satisfaction at having the harm inflicted cannot by themselves justify inflicting harm on someone. Someone might object that the example is both foolish and irrelevant because vengeance can be sought only when some ill deed has been performed, and the basketball players have done no wrong. Murderers have done wrong, and that is why revenge against them is justified.

This reply is plausible insofar as it emphasizes that vengeance must always be a response to some perceived injury or bad act, but it does not save the argument from vengeance. Suppose that the basketball players disgraced their city by playing extremely badly in a tournament or by accepting bribes and purposely losing a championship. In this case, the intense hatred and desire for harm would result from some wrong actions, but it would still not follow that the revenge sought by irate fans would be justified. At the least, executing the players would violate the proportionality principle. The fact that citizens are so angry that they would like to see the basketball players die would not justify executing them, even though they have done something wrong.

The reply is also flawed because it assumes that the desire for revenge must always be a response to some wrongful act, but in fact a person need not do anything wrong in order to inspire vengeful feelings in another. A corrupt politician may seek revenge against the reporter who exposed his wrongdoing and brought his political career to an end. The reporter did in fact cause harm to the politician, and the politician genuinely desires revenge. The politician's hatred is real, his desire that the reporter suffer is deeply felt, and he would gain genuine satisfaction from the reporter's suffering. His acts of vengeance, however, would not be justified because the reporter has done no wrong.

What these examples show is that the desire to inflict harm for ill deeds does not justify inflicting harm. There is nothing wrong with desiring that people get what they deserve or that they be justly punished. In such cases, however, it is justice that justifies punishment, not vengeance. When vengeance conflicts with justice, as it does with the desire to kill the dishonest basketball players or to harm the innocent reporter, then justice overrides revenge. So, the desire for revenge is either overridden by considerations of justice or it adds nothing to the arguments for punishment that appeal to justice.

Arguments from vengeance face a dilemma. Either they turn out to be another name for arguments from justice, in which case they add nothing to the debate about the death penalty. Or they are genuinely different from the appeal to justice, in which case, they seem to provide nothing more than an appeal to strong emotions. Yet strong emotions by themselves do not justify inflicting grave harms on others.

Executions and the Control of Vengeance

One might argue that although the desire for vengeance does not by itself justify the death penalty or any other punishment for crime, nonetheless, when such desires are widespread, the government must take them seriously. If there is a widespread desire for vengeance and this desire is not satisfied, then people will take the law into their own hands. There will be a breakdown of public order.

In a famous remark, James Fitzjames Stephen, a prominent 19th-century English judge and legal theorist, wrote that "The criminal law stands to the passion of revenge in much the same relation as marriage to the sexual appetite."[1] Developing this idea, Ernest van den Haag notes that the abolition of punishment would be no more likely to reduce the desire for revenge than the abolition of marriage would be likely to diminish sexual desires. He then warns:

> When legal retribution is not imposed for what is felt to be wrong, or when retribution is felt to be less than deserved— when it is felt to be insufficient, not inclusive, certain, or severe enough—public control falters, and the "passion for revenge" tends to be gratified privately.[2]

Although van den Haag is talking about the need for punishment generally and not about the death penalty specifically, his point is certainly applicable to the death penalty. The concern voiced here is not that the desire for revenge is legitimate but rather that, legitimate or not, if it is not satisfied, people will take the law into their own hands through vigilante justice. One way or another, this desire must be gratified. If it is not gratified in a public, controlled fashion, then it will be gratified in a private, uncontrolled manner.

The breakdown of the social order and the encouragement of vigilante justice are surely things to worry about. And there is no doubt that if there is a widespread feeling that government is not acting as it ought, this may lead to a crisis in confidence and less inclination to obey the law. If these ill effects could be predicted as consequences of abolishing the death penalty, they would have to be taken seriously.

While this argument shows that there might be cause to worry, it does not show that the government ought to execute people simply to maintain public confidence in the law. Even if we could predict the worrisome consequences described here, we might want the government to resist the calls for vengeance rather than to give in to them. In any case, there is no reason to believe that these dire consequences are likely to result from abolishing the death penalty. They might result if murderers were not punished at all or if they were given extremely lenient sentences. However, it is hard to imagine that this breakdown would occur if murderers were given long-term prison sentences. It is hard to imagine people believing that someone serving a prison sentence of twenty-five years had gotten off lightly. Punishments need not be as severe as everyone wishes in order for them to gain social acceptance.

In any case, there is no historical evidence for the thesis that fewer executions lead to more lynchings. Indeed, the opposite seems to be the case. In the 1890s, there were many executions in the United States—over 1,200. Yet there were many lynchings as well—over 1,500. Executions per decade decreased somewhat in the 1900s and 1910s while at the same time the number of lynchings diminished sharply, down to about 600 for the 1910s. Both executions and lynchings declined in number. The decline in lynchings is strongly correlated with the centralization of legal authority and the shift of authority to execute from local to state officials. Local justice seems to have been more conducive to lynching, and in the heyday of local justice, there were both many executions and many lynchings.[3] By the 1940s and 1950s, executions were declining further, and lynchings ceased almost entirely.

It is important to remember, too, that even if public dissatisfaction with punishments less severe than death does threaten to produce bad consequences, there are other ways for governments to deal with this problem. Since lynchers and vigilantes are themselves perpetrators of illegal violence, they should be dealt with severely (though not by execution) as a way of deterring others. It is not as if the only thing that government officials can do is to give in to the desire for vengeance. Nor is that what they ought to do.

Finally, before leaving this point, it is worth considering another form of the argument for public vengeance. If the public genuinely wants vengeance, then it might be argued that a respect for democratic values and procedures requires that their desire be acted upon. If a majority of citizens genuinely want the death penalty in order to avenge the deaths of murder victims, then the death penalty ought to be enforced.

This appeal to democracy confuses two different issues. One is whether a particular punishment is a wise and just policy. The other is whether a particular punishment ought to be part of the legal system if it has broad support and is therefore enacted into law by legislative bodies. One can have great respect for democratic procedures without giving up one's power of independent judgment and one's right to believe that the majority view is foolish or immoral. In addition, while respect for democratic values generally commits one to favoring enforcement of laws when they are supported by the majority and passed by legislatures, this by itself does not even guarantee the legality of a practice. Since laws may violate the Constitution, it is open to people to express their opposition through appeals to the judiciary. All of this is consistent with democracy.

Similarly, when the majority holds a view that one believes is mistaken, then democratic traditions encourage dissent and the offering of reasons for change. Democracy does not require total deference to the will of the majority. One may consistently believe that majority rule is the best form of political procedure without being committed to the idea that whatever the majority wants is best. Indeed, in the light of widespread ignorance of facts and lack of intelligent debate on many serious issues, one may be quite pessimistic about the trustworthiness of popularly accepted beliefs.

Vigilantism

Suppose one grants that the arguments we have considered show that governments ought not to engage in the execution of criminals. Might it nonetheless be true that *individuals* could be justified in seeking revenge? Would an individual person be justified in killing the murderer of someone he loved or respected?

In considering this question, it is important to distinguish the moral problem involved here from the question about legal policy. We need to consider both whether the law should regard killing a murderer as a crime, an act of murder itself, and whether such a killing is an immoral act. Let us begin by assuming that such killings are morally justified and see what follows about legal policy.

Even if people were morally justified in killing murderers, it is pretty clear that the law cannot permit such actions. A central function of government is the enforcement of laws, and a government cannot abdicate this function. Surely, governments can share some of their enforcement rights with private security agencies or other auxiliaries to its operations. It cannot, however, give to each and every citizen the right to judge and punish criminals. That is a sure route to chaos.

The problems that would arise from private enforcement of the law are precisely those that John Locke, in his *Second Treatise of Government*, noted as one of the crucial reasons for having a government. Locke thought that if there were no government at all, then people would have a right to punish those who violate the moral law. The results of this universal enforcement system are not attractive, however. As Locke noted,

> For everyone in that state being both judge and executioner of the law of nature, men being partial to themselves, passion and revenge is very apt to carry them too far, and with too much heat in their own cases; as well as negligence and unconcernedness, to make them too remiss in other men's.[4]

For Locke, the defects of the system of enforcement by all provide one of the best reasons for wanting a government. People would choose, he thought, to have a government in order to have the benefits of "known and indifferent" judges. Where people enforce the laws against those who have offended them, they are apt to be overly severe. This in turn will result in reprisals and continued violence.

As much as people might want the satisfaction of punishing those who have wronged them or who have wronged others and gone unpunished, authorizing people to do this would be disastrous. There would be no checks or procedures to prevent either the punishment of the innocent or the imposition of unjustly harsh punishments. There would be no "due process of law." All that would be required for one person to punish another would be a sincere belief that the second had committed a terrible crime. The avenging person would not be held to any procedure or standards for establishing guilt beyond a reasonable doubt. Nor would he be bound by standards for deciding the appropriate level of punishment. Mitigating and aggravating circumstances would not have to be considered. There would be absolutely no control on the process, and innocent persons would be sure to suffer.

In addition, this kind of private justice would be likely to invite reprisals and retaliation. Friends or relatives of those who had been victims of vengeance would seek to impose their own punishments. Everyone would have the same authorization to carry out these actions under such a system. There would be punishments for crimes, but there would be neither law nor order.

Such a condition would be both dangerous and unjust. No functioning government or reasonable legal system could possibly allow such activity to go on. Vigilantism and private vengeance cannot reasonably be permitted by law.

The Good Avenger

While it is clear that we cannot have a system that permits private vengeance, it is worth pausing to absorb some of the unpleasant implications of this fact. We can do this by imagining a case in which we would be most sympathetic to the avenging person. Suppose that someone is murdered and that the identity of the murderer is known "beyond reasonable doubt" by others.

Suppose, too, that the murder is especially dreadful and would be classified by most people among the worst sorts of killings. Yet, for some reason, the killer receives the most minimal punishment, and someone close to the victim (parent, spouse, or child) decides to kill the murderer.

I have already argued that this cannot be permitted by the law. Nonetheless, we might have a great deal of sympathy with the avenger. It might be clear to us that the avenger is a morally good person, driven to this act by anguish, outrage, and righteous indignation. Our sympathy would go out to this person, and we might think that morally his action was either justifiable or excusable, that the avenger morally deserved either no punishment or a mild punishment.

How should the law treat this case? It is evident that the law cannot simply permit such killings. Could it be very lenient in such a case, however? Certainly there are some mitigating circumstances—the emotional anguish of the person, the provocation provided by the killing of a loved one, the outrage at the light sentence imposed by the judge. These factors would lead us to modify our degree of moral blame, but they need not lead us to diminish legal penalties. For, just as the consequences of legally permitting vengeful killings are intolerable, so too are the consequences of excusing such killings or punishing them very leniently. To punish this act very leniently is to invite others to follow the example of the avenger, and the consequences are likely to be as bad as legally permitting vengeful killings. Our need to enforce social order cannot permit us to be too lenient even if we sympathize with the situation of the avenger and think that we might do the same in his or her situation.

What this situation reveals is a tension that was implicit in my earlier discussion of deserving. We tend to think that there should be a close relationship between the punishment that people morally deserve and the punishment that the law imposes on them. One might even think that the purpose of the legal system is simply to give people what they morally deserve. That is a mistake, however, and the reasons for the error are revealed by this case. Because the primary purpose of the law is protective, we must punish the good avenger relatively severely, even if we think this person is not morally blameworthy. We must do this because our general well-being would be threatened if we were to allow private vengeance or treat it as a nonserious offense. We cannot permit the motive of vengeance to be a legally valid excuse, even if we regard it as a morally valid excuse.

Of course, if many morally conscientious persons were impelled to enforce vigilante justice, that might indicate that the legal system is indeed faulty. This would be especially true if serious crimes were treated too leniently or if those who violated the rights of certain classes of people were not punished by the law at all.[5] In such cases, the avengers would be playing a role comparable to that of traditional civil disobedients, although the violence of their actions would make their acts much more difficult to justify than *civil* disobedience. In this case, however, their acts might draw attention to genuine flaws in the legal system.

While avengers might, then, have a valuable lesson for society in certain circumstances, this point does nothing to show that the death penalty is justified or necessary. If death penalty opponents were against all punishment for murder or favored only trivial punishments, then the lesson of avengers would count against them. Opponents of the death penalty, however, can favor quite severe punishments other than death, and the severity of the alternative punishments would not tend to trivialize the loss of innocent life caused by murder. Nor would it allow anyone to "get away with murder." So long as the law punishes murderers severely, good avengers would have no justified complaint with the legal system, and their acts would not indicate flaws in the system of justice.

Is Vengeful Killing Morally Right?

In considering the morality of vengeful killing, we have to keep separate the problem of assessing the morality of the *action* of vengeful killing from the morality of the *agent*. We can certainly imagine cases in which we would be very sympathetic to the vengeful killer. We might even consider the avenger to be a morally good person. This is a separate matter, however, from whether he or she acted rightly.

If we reflect on whether such actions can be right, whether we should add "killing to avenge the death of another" as a justifiable exception to the "don't kill" rule, I think we will come to see that morality must forbid such actions. The reasons for this are quite similar to the reasons why the law must condemn such actions. If morality included a general permission for people to avenge murders by death, then morality as an institution would function less well in protecting people's lives and their well-being. As Locke argued, people are not apt to be good or fair judges where their own feelings and interests have been severely wounded, and sanctioning people to act on their feelings and interests in these cases would pose a danger to all.

Even a person who was eager for vengeance would probably be unhappy to find himself in a society of many self-appointed law enforcers. However much one may sympathize with the desire for vengeance, it is quite something else to give everyone permission to be an avenger. We do not sufficiently trust everyone's judgment to favor this. Yet, the person who would grant this right only to himself would lack any justification for thinking that he had some special status that made it permissible for him to seek vengeance while others could not. If people generally cannot be permitted to avenge death by killing, then it is hard to see how any individual could claim such a right.

Killing from vengeance must be classified as an immoral act, then, even though we need not think that all who do this act are morally bad people. We might "understand" their actions, but we ought not to encourage them or approve of what they do.

Conclusions

In this chapter, I have tried to show that the desire for vengeance does not provide a ground either for the death penalty or for the justification of acts of private vengeance.

In the case of good avengers, we might be tempted to excuse such actions morally, but it does not follow that their action was morally right or that it should be legally permitted or legally excused. Even treating such actions leniently may not be possible, since the law cannot make the cost of private vengeance too low. To do so is to threaten everyone's well-being.

|10|

What If the Death Penalty Did Save Lives?

Throughout my discussion of the death penalty, I have frequently appealed to the importance of protecting people's lives, and I have claimed that this is a central function of government. The protection of human life possesses great importance whether we approach it from a moral or a political point of view. This is why the question of deterrence has figured so centrally in death penalty debates. Both sides know that the saving of lives carries a great deal of moral weight, so whether the death penalty prevents murders becomes a central concern. In chapter 2, I argued that the evidence available to us does not support the view that the death penalty provides additional protection to society. At present, then, any attempt to support the death penalty by appealing to its protective functions remains weak and unconvincing.

In spite of the importance of the deterrence factor, it is not the only factor that needs to be considered in assessing the morality of the death penalty. For this reason, I have considered many other issues and arguments in the course of this discussion. I believe that my examination of the death penalty has shown that it is not morally justified.

I can imagine someone thinking that while many of my arguments have some force, in the end the only thing that really matters is the deterrence problem. If this is true, then my case against the death penalty is at least theoretically weakened.

Suppose that the death penalty did prevent more murders than other available punishments. Would that show that it was justified, in spite of the other arguments against it? Does the entire case against the death penalty ultimately rest on the lack of evidence for its superior deterrent power? What if new evidence shows that it does have superior deterrent force? Or, suppose that it comes to possess such power in the future? Would the death penalty then be morally legitimate? Does the whole issue turn on facts about deterrence?

Deterrence and Morality

I would not deny that if the death penalty prevented murders more successfully than other punishments, this would be a powerful argument in its favor. To grant this, however, is not the same as saying that deterrence is the only relevant factor or that it is by itself decisive. The morality of the death penalty, like the morality of many other acts and policies, depends on many diverse factors. For this reason, many different sorts of reasons bear on our assessment of it. We cannot deduce the moral rightness or wrongness of the death penalty from just one general principle, not even from a plausible principle like "protect innocent life whenever possible." Nonetheless, if the death penalty were a superior deterrent, that would introduce a very weighty moral consideration into the balance of reasons, and the greater its deterrent power (the more lives it could be credited with saving), the weightier that reason would be.

In spite of this, it is easy to see that evidence of superior deterrent power would not by itself show that the death penalty was morally legitimate. We can see this by imagining some punishment that it is plausible to believe would be an extremely effective deterrent and yet that we would regard as immoral in spite of the fact that it saved lives.

Imagine, for example, that we were to adopt a policy of punishing murderers by administering prolonged and extraordinarily painful forms of torture, to be followed by eventual execution. Instead of aiming for "humane" forms of execution, we would select the most awful forms of execution in the belief that the more awful the process, the more powerful the deterrent. It is certainly plausible to believe that this sort of policy would have greater deterrent power than the death penalty as now administered. (It might also stimulate violence, as the brutalization hypothesis suggests, but we can leave this possibility aside for the sake of our thought experiment.) Even if this form of punishment were remarkably successful as a deterrent, I doubt that we would think that it was morally permissible to impose it. Such a punishment would require extraordinary callousness to administer, and we would surely condemn it as barbaric.

Or, suppose we adopted the following punishment for murder. We would execute not only the person who committed the murder but also the three people in the world who were of greatest personal significance to the murderer. We could imagine a post-conviction hearing in which a report was presented, assessing the murderer's relationship to other people and concluding with a judgment about which three people meant the most to the murderer. All of them would then be executed. If we were solely interested in making potential murderers "think twice," this policy would probably work much better than the death penalty as currently practiced. Yet, again, this particular practice would be truly abhorrent, and it would remain abhorrent, even if it saved more lives than other punishments.

What these examples show is that superior deterrent power is not the only issue. A punishment may save more lives and yet involve society in such ghastly practices that we would reject it as immoral.

To establish in principle that a punishment with superior deterrent power may be immoral is a matter of considerable significance. Nonetheless, by itself, it does not show that the death penalty is sufficiently ghastly to merit rejection. The death penalty would qualify as sufficiently bad in itself to be rejected by the absolute pacifist, for whom all killing is immoral, or by the person who finds executions inherently barbaric. These reactions, however, are not widely shared. Most people believe that killing is morally permissible in some circumstances, and most people think that executions can be carried out in a way that is sufficiently humane to bring them within the bounds of civility. I am not sure that the second of these judgments is correct, but I see no effective way to argue against it.[1]

I will not then try to argue that executions are on a par with torture or with the practice of executing those whom murderers care about. Rather, having shown that superior deterrent power by itself would not guarantee the morality of punishing by death, I want to see whether there are other factors that would call into question the morality of executions, even if executions were the most effective way to save lives.

Executing the Innocent

One of the most powerful objections to the death penalty arises from the possibility of executing innocent people. I take it that we would not *knowingly* execute innocent people even if this had a positive deterrent effect on the homicide rate. If this is true, then we should be deeply disturbed if we could predict that, under a death penalty system, we would unintentionally execute innocent persons. If we could predict that among the effects of instituting the death penalty would be the execution of innocent persons, this would count heavily against the death penalty, even if we could predict that another effect would be a decrease in the homicide rate.

The problem of executing the innocent is, at a certain level, quite simple. Executing innocent people would be a dreadful effect of the death penalty, and it would not be a possible effect of long term imprisonment, a possible alternative to executions. Hence, we could have a severe punishment that did not threaten to result in our killing innocent people. To maintain the death penalty is to be willing to risk innocent lives.

No one could dismiss the relevance or force of this argument, and no one could deny that executing innocent persons is a terrible act. Nonetheless, this argument raises extraordinarily difficult issues of what has sometimes been called "moral arithmetic." There would be no problem, of course, if the number of innocent people executed were larger than the number of innocent lives saved. Nor, I take it, would there be a problem if the numbers were equal. But, the issue becomes much murkier in the situation in which more innocent lives are saved by deterrence than are lost through erroneous executions.

Suppose that there were a net gain in lives saved but that the number of lives saved was extremely small. Then, I think, we would reject the death penalty and forgo the added deterrence it provides. Our decision would be supported by the idea that it is worse for us actually to kill innocent people than it is for us to fail to prevent the deaths of innocent people. The moral significance of the distinction between the harms we cause and those we fail to prevent has been called into question by some recent thinkers.[2] Nonetheless, we generally do distinguish between failing to save a life (say, by not contributing to famine relief) and actually killing someone (by taking away his food, for example). While the failure to protect is morally bad, the active killing seems much worse. So, if innocents are to die, it is better that we not be the agents of their deaths.

If, however, the number of innocents likely to be executed by mistake is very small and the number of potential homicide victims whose lives can be saved is very large, then we might well conclude that morality requires us to execute murderers. If this were our judgment, we would then be under a great deal of pressure to try to specify what "very large" and "very small" mean in this context. How many lives must be saved by executions in order for us to be justified in accepting the death penalty, even though we know that some innocent people will be executed?

I fear that I have nothing very helpful to say about how to approach the "moral arithmetic" in this case.

Nonetheless, I think we can reach several conclusions related to the problem of executing innocent people. First, if the death penalty is to be justified, we must have good reason to believe that our system is on the whole quite reliable and that very few innocent people will ever be executed. We must do our utmost to provide stringent safeguards that will make such executions highly unlikely—even if this means bearing extra legal costs, putting up with long delays, and sometimes seeing death sentences overturned for what appear to be merely "legal technicalities." Moreover, we must be confident that these safeguards will work.

Second, we must have reason to believe that the number of lives saved is *substantial*. Superior deterrent power cannot mean simply that a few lives are likely to be saved. If we assume that some innocents will be executed and that it is worse for us actively to kill a person than it is for us to fail in our efforts to prevent someone's death, then executions can be justified only if they lead to substantial savings of lives.

Finally, it must be the case that there are no feasible, morally preferable alternatives to the death penalty, no policies that are available to us and that would be equally effective in saving these innocent lives. If there were other morally acceptable policies that did not involve the possibility of executing innocents and yet that were as effective in preventing murders, then we would be morally bound to try these alternatives. If it turned out, for example, that homicide rates could be lowered through greater controls on the availability of guns, or if homicide rates are related to unemployment rates so that lowering unemployment would (along with its other benefits) lower the homicide rate, then it would be our duty to adopt these alternatives to the death penalty. It would be immoral for us to adopt the death penalty if we could predict that some innocent people would be executed and if we knew that alternative policies could save lives equally well.

Executing Innocents—A Real Problem?

The problem of executing innocent people is not imaginary or purely hypothetical. The most thorough study available on the execution of innocents has recently been carried out by Hugo Bedau and Michael Radelet.[3] They claim to have found that for the period 1900 to 1980, about 350 people were wrongfully convicted of capital offenses. Of these, 139 were sentenced to death, and twenty-three were actually executed.

These figures may be reassuring to some. One might react by thinking that the number of errors is small and that most of those wrongfully convicted were not after all executed. Somehow, it might be thought, the system was able to correct these errors in time. A closer look is less reassuring, however, for the evidence that led to a particular person's escaping execution has usually appeared by chance or resulted from the efforts of people outside the legal process. Only in thirty-seven cases, about 10 percent of the cases, were errors discovered by officials. Moreover, as time passes and with the death of those executed, further evidence regarding their cases becomes increasingly difficult to gather. It is plausible to suppose that unknown cases remain and that the number of innocent persons executed is larger than the twenty-three that Bedau and Radelet have verified.

In this connection, it is worth recalling one recent case in which an innocent person barely escaped execution. I have generally tried to avoid discussion of individual cases here so as to focus directly on the most general issues of principle. Nonetheless, an important element in the issue is the degree of confidence that we have in the efficiency, reliability, and integrity of the criminal justice system. Popular opinion seems to hold that our system is, if anything, too fair to defendants, giving them every possible opportunity to establish their innocence, while at the same time handicapping the efforts of officials to enforce the law. This is not born out by the Bedau and Radelet study. According to them, eighty-four cases of erroneous conviction resulted from questionable actions by police officers and prosecutors. Nonetheless, most people seem confident that if a trial and appeals have occurred and a person's death sentence remains standing, then he must be guilty and his execution must at least be legally appropriate.

In a study of the death penalty in Georgia since the *Gregg* decision, Ursula Bentele reports on the case of Jerry Banks, a man who discovered two dead bodies while hunting.[4] Banks went to a road and stopped a car, asking the driver to report the deaths to the police. Banks waited for the police, and when they arrived, he led them to the bodies. One month later, Banks, a black man, was charged with the murder. He was tried, convicted, and sentenced to death, in spite of the fact that a neighbor testified that Banks had been at her home at the time when the shooting occurred. Moreover, the driver whom Banks had signaled and who phoned the police was never called as a witness, and a detective testified that he did not know his identity. In fact, this person, a Mr. Eberhardt, had left his name with the police, had made himself available to the grand jury, had spoken with the judge who conducted the trial, and had made a statement for the sheriff. The Supreme Court of Georgia, in ordering a new trial, specifically noted that the sheriff and other officers knew the identity of this witness but "either intentionally or inadvertently" kept it from Banks and his lawyer.

Banks was tried a second time and again convicted and sentenced to death, apparently because of ineffective work by his lawyer. Only after this second death sentence did two new attorneys discover evidence that the murder weapon could not have been Banks's hunting rifle. They found witnesses who had reported hearing rapid fire shots that could not have come from Banks's shotgun. Others reported that they had seen two white men arguing shortly before the murder took place. Several of the witnesses had actually reported what they had seen to the police, but the reports were ignored and were not introduced at Banks's second trial.

In a second appeal, Banks again won a new trial. This time, after seven years of legal proceedings stretching from 1974 through 1981, all charges against him were dropped.

While this case may not be typical, the Bedau-Radelet study shows that it is far from unique. The occurrence of such cases is sufficient to call into question our confidence that the awesome responsibility of dealing with crimes that may lead to execution is treated with appropriate care by officials. In the Banks case, physical evidence and witnesses' reports were lost, neglected, or suppressed. If the new attorneys had not intervened on his behalf after the second trial, he would have been executed, and the error might never have come to light.

In considering the problem of executing innocent people, then, we are not dealing with a merely hypothetical problem. With the best will in the world, our system will make mistakes. What Bentele's description of the Banks case and the Bedau-Radelet study clearly indicate is that we cannot count on the best will in the world being exercised by those involved in prosecuting and judging people accused of murder. This is a distressing but important fact about the criminal justice system.

Other Wrongful Executions

A person can be wrongfully executed even if he or she actually did kill someone. As we have already seen, neither morality nor the law treats all killings as equally bad. In order to determine that a person has committed the type of killing for which the law sanctions execution, the crime must be distinguished from other killings that are not capital offenses. Finally, even after conviction for first degree murder, difficult issues concerning mitigating and aggravating circumstances must be considered.

I have already discussed these issues in chapter 4 and will not enter into detailed discussion of them here.[5] Nonetheless, when we are toting up the costs of the death penalty, we need to include not only the execution of those who were factually innocent of any crime whatever but also those cases in which the accused were guilty of a killing but nonetheless did not satisfy the legal criteria for execution. We need to recall as well the haziness of these criteria and the resulting fact that many who have been condemned to die would not strike most people as those who were most deserving of death.[6]

That wrongful executions of this sort occur is perhaps best revealed by the history of punishments for rape. While rape is a very serious crime, most people would not think that punishment by death is morally required for it. A similar judgment was reached by the Supreme Court in 1977. It ruled that execution is a disproportionately severe punishment for the crime of rape and thus constitutes a cruel and unusual punishment. Nonetheless, between 1930 and 1964, 455 people—90 percent of whom were black—were executed for rape in the United States.[7]

Even in the case of killings, the facts are complicated, and leniency and severity in sentencing are the products of numerous factors, many of them irrelevant to the nature of the crime. There is no reason to believe that our system will cease to be arbitrary and discriminatory in these ways. Even a death penalty system that deterred murders and hence saved more lives than one that imposed imprisonment alone would continue to be flawed by uneven justice. As long as racial, class, religious, and economic bias continue to be important determinants of who is executed, the death penalty will both create and perpetuate injustice.

To recall an earlier example, imagine that 100 executions per year save more lives than no executions at all. Imagine further that of all those convicted of murder, the only ones who are executed have red hair. Consider how such people would regard the criminal justice system. Or, to bring home the point, imagine that instead of red heads, those executed are always members of some group (racial, ethnic, religious, or professional) to which you belong. Each of us would be deeply disturbed by such a pattern. We would feel strongly that members of our group were being treated unjustly, that our lives were not being treated as significant, that we alone were paying the price for added deterrence. Yet because of our increased exposure to executions, we would be gaining less from the decrease in homicide rates. Whatever the target group might be, this practice would be an expression of the strongest contempt and lack of regard for its members. The injustice would be obvious.

All of the defects of such an arbitrary system remain and continue to constitute a serious objection to the death penalty.

Even if it were a more effective deterrent than imprisonment, an arbitrarily administered death penalty would be morally unjust, and it would be cruel and unusual in the sense affirmed by the Supreme Court in *Furman v. Georgia*.

Deterrence in the Abstract

Philosophers are especially fond of "what if?" questions. Such questions allow us to alter factual contingencies and are sometimes helpful in revealing the principles that underlie our judgments. So, let us ask, "What if the deterrent power of the death penalty were so great that it would be extremely difficult to deny its use?"

Suppose, for example, that every execution of a person for murder saved 10,000 lives. If that were the effect of the death penalty, it would be difficult for almost all of us to deny that it was justified, even if it possessed all the defects I have described. What does this show?

One might think that it shows that the death penalty is theoretically justifiable and hence that it offends no deep principles. If the world were a little different and the death penalty were more clearly a superior deterrent, then it would be morally permissible.

I think that this conclusion is mistaken. In this instance, the "what if?" question and the imaginary case of saving thousands by killing one are not helpful. They distort our thinking about the death penalty rather than helping to clarify it. We can see the distorting effects of the example by noting that we could construct a similar argument for the view that there is nothing deeply wrong with executing purely innocent people. Suppose that by executing a person who was totally innocent of any crime, we could get the same life-saving effects. Kill one innocent person— perhaps in a gruesome, torturous manner—and 10,000 others who would have been murder victims will be spared.

Even if we were to decide that executing an innocent person was the morally best thing to do *in this situation*, that would do nothing to show that knowingly executing innocent persons is not fundamentally wrong in our world. It would not show that if only things were a little different, executing innocent persons would be permissible. So, likewise, the fact that we can imagine the death penalty having extreme life-protecting powers does not show that it is not deeply defective in our world. It does not show that the only thing that matters is deterrence.

In this instance, stretching our imaginations may have the effect of breaking down our ability to make a moral assessment. Our moral understanding breaks down here because we have a clash between the prohibition against performing a ghastly act, an act that is a paradigm of immorality, and the injunction that we perform an act that will result in the saving of many, many lives. Where the stakes are so high, the gains on one side so great, it may be that any moral rule or principle can be overwhelmed. Yet, this does nothing to show that in normal circumstances, we ought to treat these principles as if they had no moral importance.

Such examples are in the end totally irrelevant to our reflections about the death penalty.[8] In our world, the system of law and punishment does not operate in this way. No magical and extraordinary effects flow from the punishment of individual criminals. Rather, there are numerous actions that involve many different people, and it is the patterns formed by these actions that have overall social effects like the deterrence of homicide. It is the pattern of treatment of criminals that serves to deter. Likewise, it is the pattern of how we treat even those who violate the laws that reveals the extent to which concerns for justice and human dignity play a part in our lives.

It is highly unlikely that the death penalty will ever operate so effectively as to save many more lives than other, less severe punishments. Yet, given its defects, it would have to save many more lives in order for it to be a genuine candidate for moral legitimacy. If it had this positive effect, we would be faced with an anguished choice, just as we would be faced with an anguished choice if we found that executing innocent people saved many lives. Fortunately, all of this is merely hypothetical. We have no reason to believe that the death penalty does save more lives than other punishments, and so we need not actually confront this choice.

Conclusions

In this chapter, I have tried to respond to the view that deterrence is the only genuine issue in the death penalty debate.

Someone who believes this will be led to think that even if all other arguments against the death penalty are correct, the case against the death penalty would be totally undermined by evidence that the death penalty does possess superior deterrent power.

I have tried to show that this view is mistaken, while at the same time acknowledging the moral force of the appeal to saving lives. I have tried to show that some punishments are so dreadful that we would forsake them even if they saved lives, that the death penalty would remain flawed by the possibility of wrongful executions, that the problem of wrongful executions is not merely hypothetical, that arbitrary and discriminatory imposition of the death penalty would remain serious moral defects in the system. The number of lives saved would have to be extremely substantial in order to offset these defects.

Since none of us believes that all is permitted whenever saving lives is at issue, one could consistently and reasonably oppose the death penalty even if it had these life-saving powers. Fortunately for death penalty opponents, the death penalty has not been shown to save lives, so they do not have to face the anguished choices I have described. Rather, the shoe is on the other foot. Death penalty supporters are in the position of defending a system that has all of these serious flaws and that apparently fails to provide any additional protection of people's lives or well-being.

|11|

The Death Penalty as a Symbolic Issue

T HE DEBATE ABOUT the morality of the death penalty is one of those recurring questions that seems to have a life of its own. Shifts in public opinion, actions by legislatures, or decisions by courts may sometimes appear to put the issue to rest, but somehow the debate retains its vigor. Why is this?

The first and perhaps most important reason is the obvious one that lives are at stake. Death penalty opponents cannot accept defeat because the operation of the death penalty means that people will die. Some of those who die ought not to be executed, even if we accept the criteria of death penalty supporters. They may be innocent, or they may have acted wrongly but not from deep-seated malice or cruelty. To let the issue rest is to allow these errors to occur without challenge. Likewise, for death penalty supporters who believe that executions are a superior deterrent, it is the lives of potential victims that are at stake. They too cannot rest when public policy runs contrary to their views.

Second, because the stakes are high, people's feelings are deeply engaged by the issue, and they are motivated to continue the struggle. The taking of lives—whether by murder or by legal execution—is a "gut" issue, not in the sense that we cannot reason about it but rather in the sense that we are deeply affected by killings and feel strongly about the views we hold. Given the strong feelings aroused by the issue, neither side is willing to accept defeat.

Finally, the question whether we ought to punish by death is a question with great symbolic meaning. For people on both sides, whether we impose or refrain from imposing the death penalty seems to say something about our values, about the kind of people we are, about the nature of our society. The death penalty debate is in part a field on which we champion some of our most central social and ethical ideals. We think that retaining or abolishing the death penalty conveys an important message, and we want it to be the right message.

One might think that symbolic messages are even more difficult to reason about than the other questions we have considered, but there is no obvious reason why assessing these messages is beyond our ability. If they are an important component of the debate, we should try to confront them directly.

The Courage of Our Convictions

Commenting on the motivation of death penalty opponents, Ernest van den Haag has described opposition to executions as rooted in a kind of weakness of the will, an inability to overcome fears and doubts in order to act decisively in the face of evil. Describing those who oppose the death penalty, he writes:

> [T]hose who affect such a view do so because of a failure of nerve. They do not think themselves—and therefore anyone else—competent to decide questions of life and death. Aware of human frailty they shudder at the gravity of the decision and refuse to make it. The irrevocability of a verdict of death is contrary to the modern spirit that likes to pretend that nothing is ever definitive, that everything is open-ended, that doubts must always be entertained and revisions made. Such an attitude may be proper for inquiring philosophers and scientists. But not for the courts. They can evade decisions on life and death only by giving up their paramount duties: to do justice, to secure the lives of the citizens, and to vindicate the norms society holds inviolable.[1]

The rhetoric of this passage is powerful, as it draws its strength from a number of important ideals. Since no opponent of the death penalty would deny the value of doing justice, securing the lives of citizens, and vindicating important social norms, van den Haag thinks that it can only be a kind of moral squeamishness that leads them to oppose the death penalty. They are unable to support doing the unpleasant, even when it is morally required.

If van den Haag is correct about what motivates opposition to the death penalty, then his analysis might have some force in discrediting the opposition. Although it is an *ad hominem* argument, it would be important if it could be shown that only this sort of motivation could lead to opposing the death penalty. This in itself is an implausible claim, however, and indeed, none of the specific charges he makes necessarily applies to death penalty opponents.

It is not true, for example, that death penalty opponents need think of themselves as being incompetent to make life-and-death decisions. Anyone who believes that it is morally permissible to kill in self-defense is willing to sanction a life-and-death decision. Moreover, anyone who believes that the right to kill to defend oneself or others implies the legitimacy of authorizing police officers to carry weapons and to use them when necessary is clearly willing to grant the making of life-and-death decisions to other people. Anyone who believes that there can be morally just participation in war is willing to make and allow precisely these decisions. All of these positions sanction the use of deadly force, and they are all compatible with opposition to the death penalty. Opponents of the death penalty need not deny the legitimacy or necessity of killing in defense of people's lives. They may grant this, while at the same time insisting that we exercise the strictest possible limitations on the taking of lives. Killing may be morally justified in many cases, but it is not justified as punishment.

It is important to see that killing itself has different meanings in different contexts. The execution of a person convicted of a crime is a violent act. Typically, it cuts short the life of the criminal against his will and with no regard for his interests or well-being. This is quite different from what happens in the case of a "mercy killing." Those who kill in this type of situation take someone's life in the belief that this accords with that person's best interests. Whatever the merits of the arguments for or against euthanasia, approval of this practice is consistent with opposition to the death penalty. Where a person favors euthanasia but opposes the death penalty, it is evident that his motivation is not an irrational fear of making life and death decisions.

So, the general disability that van den Haag claims to see in his opponents, the failure of nerve, is in no way a necessary trait in those who oppose the death penalty. One can be quite prepared to support some acts of killing and hence be as strong willed and courageous as van den Haag without thinking that punishing by death is morally legitimate.

The failure of nerve that van den Haag claims to find in death penalty opponents is linked in his mind with a tendency toward skepticism and an awareness of human frailty and fallibility. Here, there may be some justice to his claim, but the trait that he regards as a flaw is a virtue. Of course, we are frail and fallible in our judgments, and in the light of that, we ought to be most careful when we take actions with dire, irrevocable consequences. To take someone's life is a serious matter, and we ought not to do this lightly. This is not to say that we should never do it, but we want to limit such actions to the minimum, and where there is serious doubt, we may want to avoid such actions altogether.

In saying this, I do not mean that it is always wrong to kill under conditions of uncertainty. Faced with a situation in which one person appears intent on killing another without apparent justification, one might legitimately kill the first to save the apparent victim. The action might be justified even if (tragically) it turned out that one was mistaken about who was the victim and who was the attacker. The circumstance leaves no time for inquiry and no alternative actions as options.

In the case of the death penalty, however, the victim's life is unfortunately beyond recovery, and imprisonment is sufficient to insure that the killer is no longer an active threat to other members of society. In this context, faced with our knowledge of our own fallibility in making both factual judgments and moral assessments, there is nothing improper in refraining from the more drastic action involved in punishing by death.

The kind of skepticism we are talking about here is not the abstract sort of philosophical doubt that one might acquire from reading Descartes' *Meditations* or Plato's early dialogues. The skepticism of death penalty opponents is rooted in the knowledge of the imperfections of our legal system, its history of error, misjudgment, and injustice. We know that while people may speak of seeking justice and making people's lives secure and while they may even conscientiously strive to achieve these goals, their actions and judgments are influenced by many factors. The result of their pursuit may be unnecessary deaths and widespread injustice. Given the facts of human history, skeptical worries about the correctness of the life-and-death decisions involved in punishing by death are quite legitimate.

By all means, let us be decisive when we can act to protect ourselves and others from victimization. But at the same time, let us be aware of our weaknesses and the defects of our institutions, and let us temper our actions and policies in the light of this knowledge. A bit of skepticism in this context is quite appropriate and need not reflect any moral or character weakness in opponents of the death penalty.

The Morality of Anger

The symbolic importance of the death penalty is strongly emphasized by Walter Berns in his defense of the death penalty. In discussing the symbolism of punishing by death, Berns stresses the moral significance of anger. He writes:

If . . . men are not angry when someone else is robbed, raped, or murdered, the implication is that no moral community exists, because those men do not care for anyone other than themselves. Anger is an expression of that caring, and society needs men who care for one another....[Anger] is the passion that can cause us to act for reasons having nothing to do with selfish or mean calculation; indeed, when educated, it can become a generous passion, the passion that protects the community or country by demanding punishment for its enemies.[2]

Berns wants to vindicate anger because he regards it as an expression of concern for others, and he fears that society is being undermined by a lack of other-directed concerns. He criticizes liberal political theory for what he sees as a capitulation to self-interest. Anger shows that we are not simply self-interested individuals joined together in a marriage of convenience. Instead, we are a community of people who share common concerns and recognize common values.

Berns is certainly correct that anger may reveal important virtues in people, especially if a failure to be angry arises either from callousness or indifference. Nonetheless, whatever virtues are displayed by anger, everyone would agree that the actions that flow from anger must be controlled. The expression of anger needs to be limited by moral constraints, and the reasons for these constraints are moral and not simply pragmatic or self-interested.

A person whose family has been killed in an automobile accident caused by the carelessness of another driver may be angry enough to kill the driver. The anger shows the depth of the person's caring for other human beings, but it does not provide a justification for killing the driver. Virtually everyone would agree that execution for carelessness is too severe a response. While some negative response to destructive and harmful actions is appropriate, it does not follow that anything done in the name of righteous anger is morally right.

I know of no one who denies that anger and outrage are the appropriate responses to the murder of innocent human beings. Nor do I know of anyone who argues that murderers should not be punished at all. The question is whether punishing by death is morally required. That we may feel angry enough to kill someone does not imply that doing so would be morally legitimate.

So, one can sympathize and agree with much of Berns' message, but that message does nothing to support the appropriateness of using death as a punishment. To favor severe but lesser punishments is in no way to express indifference or callousness toward the deaths of murder victims. The anger and grief that we feel about these deaths do not give us a license to kill.

Indeed, at the level of symbolism, one would think that it was important to convey the message that strong feelings of anger or hatred do not by themselves justify the taking of life. In a society where the strength of one's passions became a justification for harming others (and not just a potential excuse or mitigating factor), those whom we care about would be more rather than less threatened. It would be a mistake to convey to people that killing in anger is a morally acceptable act.

Affirming the Moral Order

Berns is critical of liberal political theorists because they emphasize that government is a humanly created instrument. He believes that if people regard laws as conveniences for improving life, then they will not take them seriously enough. They will feel free to disobey the law when obedience is inconvenient. Part of the appeal of the death penalty for Berns is that it suggests that the law possesses a transcendent value. "Capital punishment," he writes,

> serves to remind us of the majesty of the moral order that is embodied in our law and of the terrible consequences of its breach. The law must not be understood to be merely statute that we enact or repeal at our will and obey or disobey at our convenience, especially not the criminal law. . . . The criminal law must be made awful, by which I mean, awe-inspiring. . . . It must remind us of the moral order by which alone we can live as *human* beings, and in our day the only punishment that can do this is capital punishment.[3]

For Berns, permitting the state to punish by death is a means of affirming the moral order and its embodiment in the law.

Berns is correct about one point here. The law must support the moral order in the sense that it must provide appropriate punishments for particular crimes. Morality is subverted when terrible crimes go unpunished or are punished very leniently, since these responses would suggest that the crimes are not really serious. One of the worst implications of the statistics that show fewer death sentences for murders of black victims is that this undermines the value of the lives of black citizens and sends a permissive signal to people about the killing of blacks.

In the same way, however, the disproportionate number of blacks who have been executed for killing whites seriously calls into question Berns' notion that the actual practice of the death penalty affirms the moral order. Berns' romantic vision of the death penalty cannot withstand confrontation with the actual practice of executions. The actual history of the death penalty is scarcely an ennobling spectacle.

Thinking about the actual practice of executions as opposed to a romanticized vision of what punishment might be leads to the most serious problem with Berns' view of the symbolism of executions. Berns wants to see the moral order reaffirmed, but he equates this order with the legal system. He does not want us to view the law "merely [as] statute that we enact or repeal at will." Yet, that is precisely what the law is. While the moral order does not shift with the votes of a legislature, the legal order does. All too frequently, the legal order itself runs quite counter to what morality would require. Berns does the cause of morality no service by offering a blanket sanctification of the law.

Surely Berns is correct in his view that the nature and content of the law is a serious matter, but it is doubtful that we need to kill people in order to convey that message. Moreover, by revering the law when it does not deserve reverence, we help to perpetuate injustice. A critical and sober view of the law may do more to affirm the moral order than an attitude of awe or exaggerated respect. The critic who sees the flaws of the legal system and wants to limit its powers may be as committed to the moral order as Berns and may indeed have a better way to make the legal system conform to the moral order.

There are, then, several flaws in Berns' argument. He nowhere shows that the death penalty is necessary to producing the right moral attitude toward the law. He ignores the reality of the death penalty and the messages that its actual—as opposed to its idealized—workings convey. Finally, he supports a reverential and uncritical view of the law that is not likely to help us to improve the legal order.

The Symbolism of Abolishing the Death Penalty

What is the symbolic message that we would convey by deciding to renounce the death penalty and to abolish its use?

I think that there are two primary messages. The first is the most frequently emphasized and is usually expressed in terms of the sanctity of human life, although I think we could better express it in terms of respect for human dignity. One way we express our respect for the dignity of human beings is by abstaining from depriving them of their lives, even if they have done terrible deeds. In defense of human well-being, we may punish people for their crimes, but we ought not to deprive them of everything, which is what the death penalty does.

If we take the life of a criminal, we convey the idea that by his deeds he has made himself worthless and totally without human value. I do not believe that we are in a position to affirm that of anyone. We may hate such a person and feel the deepest anger

m, but when he no longer poses a threat to anyone, we
to take his life.

e might ask, hasn't the murderer forfeited whatever

rights he might have had to our respect? Hasn't he, by his deeds, given up any rights that he had to decent treatment? Aren't we morally free to kill him if we wish?

These questions express important doubts about the obligation to accord any respect to those who have acted so deplorably, but I do not think that they prove that any such forfeiture has occurred. Certainly, when people murder or commit other crimes, they do forfeit some of the rights that are possessed by the law-abiding. They lose a certain right to be left alone. It becomes permissible to bring them to trial and, if they are convicted, to impose an appropriate—even a dreadful—punishment on them.

Nonetheless, they do not forfeit all their rights. It does not follow from the vileness of their actions that we can do anything whatsoever to them. This is part of the moral meaning of the constitutional ban on cruel and unusual punishments. No matter how terrible a person's deeds, we may not punish him in a cruel and unusual way. We may not torture him, for example. His right not to be tortured has not been forfeited. Why do these limits hold? Because this person remains a human being, and we think that there is something in him that we must continue to respect in spite of his terrible acts.

One way of seeing why those who murder still deserve some consideration and respect is by reflecting again on the idea of what it is to *deserve* something. In most contexts, we think that what people deserve depends on what they have done, intended, or tried to do. It depends on features that are qualities of individuals. The best person for the job deserves to be hired. The person who worked especially hard deserves our gratitude. We can call the concept that applies in these cases *personal* desert.

There is another kind of desert, however, that belongs to people by virtue of their humanity itself and does not depend on their individual efforts or achievements. I will call this impersonal kind of desert *human* desert. We appeal to this concept when we think that everyone deserves a certain level of treatment no matter what their individual qualities are. When the signers of the Declaration of Independence affirmed that people had inalienable rights to "life, liberty, and the pursuit of happiness," they were appealing to such an idea. These rights do not have to be earned by people. They are possessed "naturally," and everyone is bound to respect them.

According to the view that I am defending, people do not lose all of their rights when they commit terrible crimes. They still deserve some level of decent treatment simply because they remain living, functioning human beings. This level of moral desert need not be earned, and it cannot be forfeited. This view may sound controversial, but in fact everyone who believes that cruel and unusual punishment should be forbidden implicitly agrees with it. That is, they agree that even after someone has committed a terrible crime, we do not have the right to do anything whatsoever to him.

What I am suggesting is that by renouncing the use of death as a punishment, we express and reaffirm our belief in the inalienable, unforfeitable core of human dignity.

Why is this a worthwhile message to convey? It is worth conveying because this belief is both important and precarious. Throughout history, people have found innumerable reasons to degrade the humanity of one another. They have found qualities in others that they hated or feared, and even when they were not threatened by these people, they have sought to harm them, deprive them of their liberty, or take their lives from them. They have often felt that they had good reasons to do these things, and they have invoked divine commands, racial purity, and state security to support their deeds.

These actions and attitudes are not relics of the past. They remain an awful feature of the contemporary world. By renouncing the death penalty, we show our determination to accord at least minimal respect even to those whom we believe to be personally vile or morally vicious. This is, perhaps, why we speak of the *sanctity* of human life rather than its value or worth. That which is sacred remains, in some sense, untouchable, and its value is not dependent on its worth or usefulness to us. Kant expressed this ideal of respect in the famous second version of the Categorical Imperative: "So act as to treat humanity, whether in thine own person or in that of any other, in every case as an end withal, never as a means only."[4]

The Problem of Moral Monsters

One may feel attracted to this ideal and yet resist it by calling to mind people like Hitler or Stalin or their various henchmen, who were responsible for the deaths of millions of innocent people.

Aren't such people beyond the pale? Haven't they forfeited *all* claims to even minimal decency so that it would be appropriate to execute them as punishment for their deeds? Doesn't the existence of such people show that the death penalty is legitimate?

These troubling questions raise important issues, and death penalty opponents might meet them in diverse ways. For myself, I am willing to say that even in these cases, so long as these people no longer pose an active threat to others, it would be best not to execute them. Moreover, though their deeds were terrible beyond words, I think it best that we not renounce our respect for their humanity.

One reason for refusing to execute such people is that we may be misled by thinking of them as solely and entirely responsible for the terrible policies carried out under their rule. In quite important ways, it is misleading to think of Hitler and Stalin or other comparable people as the doers of the terrible deeds we associate with them. Certainly, they were agents of death and destruction, but they could not have carried out their plans without the encouragement, the complicity, and the active assistance of vast numbers of people. Had others turned a deaf ear to Hitler's nationalistic, antisemitic ravings, there would have been no Nazi party. Had other refused to work within the Nazi and Soviet bureaucracies of death, there would have been neither Holocaust nor Gulag. It is in fact too comforting to personalize these evils and lay them at the footsteps of monsters. It is too comforting to think that only a special kind of monstrous person could bring about such evil. It is both more accurate and more frightening to realize what ordinary human beings are capable of. Without the assistance of many ordinary people, Hitler and Stalin would have been quite powerless to carry out their evil wishes.

It is important, too, to realize just how selective we are in our appraisals of historic figures. Looking back, for example, we think of Napoleon as one of the great men of history. In Paris, there is an imposing monument to him at Les Invalides. Yet, Napoleon was responsible for plunging Europe into almost twenty years of war. In his Russian campaign alone, over 400,000 French soldiers died. His actions led to untold numbers of casualties and deaths. Yet he is remembered by most as a heroic figure.

Coming closer to home, the Allied forces in World War II carried out a policy of continuous, deliberate bombings of German and Japanese cities that was designed to terrorize the civilian populations. Many thousands of people were killed by these raids. This effort culminated, of course, in the atomic bombings at Hiroshima and Nagasaki. Vast numbers of innocent people were victims of these campaigns. The names of Churchill and Truman, however, remain highly honored. We do not consider them monsters.

Nor do we think of the various presidents since Harry Truman as moral monsters, though each one has apparently been willing to launch nuclear bombs that would kill millions of innocent people in retaliation against an attack on the United States. Smiling young men in missile silos report on television that of course they would push the buttons if they were given the orders to do so. Thousands of other ordinary people earn their living by designing and making the components of nuclear weapons.

None of these people are monsters, and yet all contribute to an effort whose result could be the extermination of human life. In general, however, we are not horrified by them as we are by Hitler or Stalin. We find our own officials and our fellow citizens more human, easier to identify with. We take their justifications for their acts more seriously because we share their concerns. We do not think that our military and political officials must have lost every shred of humanity in order to be involved in these efforts. Yet, the destruction they declare themselves willing to produce dwarfs that which was done by Hitler and Stalin.

My point here is not that Hitler and Stalin were not evil people. Nor do I wish to deny that there are differences between them and other leaders. What I want to draw attention to is the selective nature of our moral vision. We are horrified by the destructive deeds and intentions of some world leaders, while we take those of other leaders quite in stride. Some evil deeds strike us as indicative of no humanity in a person, while others are oddly untroubling.

It would be worth exploring the criteria by which we judge people to be moral monsters and worth trying to see what one must do in order to lose all claims to human consideration. This might be a more difficult task than many think and might well have unwelcome consequences.

What I have been trying to suggest here is that when people focus on figures like Hitler or Stalin, they often want to exhibit examples of superhuman evil. Yet, this exhibition rests on a number of comforting illusions. I find it more telling to recognize the humanity of the motives that can lead to terrible actions and to see that these motivations are not limited to the few terrible figures we tend to pick out as exemplars of evil. The appeal to the existence of moral monsters to justify executions rests on too simple a conception of the roots of evil.

Not all opponents of the death penalty would agree with the views I have expressed about figures like Hitler and Stalin, and though I regard them as important points, they are not essential to meet the original objection. The objection we were considering offered Hitler and Stalin as examples of people who had acted so vilely that they had forfeited any right to decent treatment. In their cases, it could be argued, we need not worry about imposing death, and therefore, the death penalty can be legitimate.

While I have rejected this view, it would be possible for an opponent of the death penalty to agree with the premise of this argument and to concede that Hitler and Stalin might have gone so far that they no longer merited any consideration as human beings. One could even acknowledge that they should be executed.

All of this is consistent with opposition to the death penalty. Why? Because these cases are extraordinary and atypical. The death penalty controversy is concerned with the use of death as a punishment for murders that occur within society. It is advocated as a part of our ordinary criminal justice system. One could favor executing Hitler because of his extraordinary acts and still think that executions should play no regular role in the achievement of domestic order within a society.

From the perspective of this reply, the whole issue of moral monsters is a distraction that confuses the issue. If death penalty supporters were proposing executions only for extraordinary political criminals like Hitler and Stalin, these examples would be to the point. Since they are proposing executions for people whose deeds do not begin to approach the evil of these famous persons, death penalty supporters must make a different sort of case for their view. The specter of Hitler and Stalin does not help their case at all.

The Morality of Restraint

I have argued that the first symbolic meaning conveyed by a renunciation of the death penalty is that human dignity must be respected in every person. To execute a person for murder is to treat that person as if he were nothing but a murderer and to deprive him of everything that he has. Therefore, if we want to convey the appropriate message about human dignity, we will renounce the death penalty.

One might object that, in making this point, I am contradicting my earlier claim that killing in defense of oneself or others can be morally justified. If it is wrong to execute a person because this violates his dignity as a human being and deprives him of everything, it would seem to be equally wrong to kill this person as a means of defense. Defensive killing seems to violate these ideals in the same way that I claim punishing by death does. Isn't this inconsistent? Mustn't I either retreat to the absolute pacifist view or else allow that the death penalty is permissible?

In chapter 1, I argued that defensive killing is morally permissible. What I need to do now is to show that defensive killing is compatible with respect for human dignity. We can easily see that it is by recalling the central fact about killing to ward off an assault on one's own life. In this circumstance, someone will die. The only question open is whether it will be the attacker or the intended victim. We cannot act in any way that shows the very same respect and concern for both the attacker and the intended victim. Although we have no wish to harm the attacker, this is the only way to save the innocent person who is being attacked. In this situation, assuming that there are no alternative means of preventing the attack from succeeding, it is permissible to kill the attacker.

What is crucial here is that the choice is forced on us. If we do not act, then one person will be destroyed. There is no way of showing equal concern for both attacker and victim, so we give preference to the intended victim and accept the morality of killing the attacker.

The case of punishing by death is entirely different. If this punishment will neither save the life of the victim nor prevent the deaths of other potential victims, then the decision to kill the murderer is avoidable. We can restrain ourselves without sacrificing the life or well-being of other people who are equally deserving of respect and consideration. In this situation, the restrained reaction is the morally right one.

In addition to providing an answer to the objection, this point provides us with the second important message conveyed by the renunciation of punishing by death. When we restrain ourselves and do not take the lives of those who kill, we communicate the importance of minimizing killing and other acts of violence. We reinforce the idea that violence is morally legitimate only as a defensive measure and should be curbed whenever possible.

We can see the point of this message by contrasting it with Walter Berns' emphasis on the morality of anger. Without discounting all that Berns says, it seems to me that the death penalty supports the morality of anger in an unacceptable way. It suggests that if someone's acts have provoked you to be very angry, then you may legitimately act violently against that person. The morality of restraint, on the other hand, requires that one control one's anger and allows one to attack another person only defensively. Anger by itself provides no justification for violence.

When the state has a murderer in its power and could execute him but does not, this conveys the idea that even though this person has done wrong and even though we may be angry, outraged, and indignant with him, we will nonetheless control ourselves in a way that he did not. We will not kill him, even though we could do so and even though we are angry and indignant. We will exercise restraint, sanctioning killing only when it serves a protective function.

Why should we do this? Partly out of a respect for human dignity. But also because we want the state to set an example of proper behavior. We do not want to encourage people to resort to violence to settle conflicts when there are other ways available. We want to avoid the cycle of violence that can come from retaliation and counter-retaliation. Violence is a contagion that arouses hatred and anger, and if unchecked, it simply leads to still more violence. The state can convey the message that the contagion must be stopped, and the most effective principle for stopping it is the idea that only defensive violence is justifiable. Since the death penalty is not an instance of defensive violence, it ought to be renounced.

We show our respect for life best by restraining ourselves and allowing murderers to live, rather than by following a policy of a life for a life. Respect for life and restraint of violence are aspects of the same ideal. The renunciation of the death penalty would symbolize our support of that ideal.

Conclusions

In this chapter, I have tried to interpret and evaluate several of the symbolic messages that our acceptance or renunciation of the death penalty might convey. I have tried to show that the abolition of punishing by death reflects neither cowardice nor moral indifference. Rather, it expresses a commitment to respect human dignity and to minimize the degree of permissible violence. These two tasks clearly go together. Where violence is not severely limited, human dignity is constantly violated, and human life becomes precarious.

Epilogue

In writing this book, I have tried to make as good a case as I can against the use of death as a punishment. That has not been my sole aim, however. I have also tried to give serious consideration to the concerns and arguments of those who favor the death penalty. While I believe that their support of executions is a mistake, I recognize that the impulses that motivate them may be as humane and worthy of respect as those that motivate death penalty opponents.

This is not to deny that there are people whose support of the death penalty is motivated by cruelty, hatred, or prejudice. Nor is it to deny that there are people in public life who exploit the emotional impact of this issue to their own advantage and who themselves do not care in the least about what may be morally right. Nonetheless, I very much doubt that the mass of death penalty supporters fall into either category.

In any case, it is both strategically and morally bad to begin by thinking the worst of those who disagree with us. That route leads to disrespect, failures of communication, and breakdowns of co-operation. Disagreement about moral issues and public policy decisions is itself one form of social conflict, and how we handle such conflict may have important implications for our dealing with conflict generally. Discussion and debate are devices for dealing with conflict in a nonviolent manner. The same is true of voting and other democratic procedures. These devices can work, however, only if we presuppose a certain degree of good will on the part of those who participate. Where this is lacking, power politics and the use of force become the only options.

Regrettably, force and coercion are sometimes necessary, but they should always be our last resort, and we should strive to cultivate alternative ways of dealing with conflict. Serious debate of issues, carried on in a spirit of mutual respect, is one of these alternatives that needs to be cultivated and developed. It is much easier to avoid the task, to think of our opponents as enemies and to regard our differences as beyond discussion. But we pay a heavy price for this. By adopting this perspective, we insure that those whose views we oppose will be our enemies. Likewise, by believing our differences beyond discussion and resolution, we guarantee that they will be just that. The costs can be seen in the widespread acceptance of false forms of toughness and in the pervasiveness of domestic and international violence.

In the last chapter, I argued that by renouncing the use of the death penalty, we could show our respect for human dignity and our commitment to avoiding violence whenever possible. These ideals are quite general and apply to all of our ways of dealing with conflict. It is easy (or at least easier) to be understanding of those we love and those who share our interests, concerns, and points of view. It is harder to be understanding and respectful of those with whom we differ, but these attitudes are certainly necessary for a democratic society to flourish, and they may be necessary for the survival of human society itself.

The ethics of anger and toughness have brought us to the brink of extinction. Perhaps it is time for something else—not an absolute renunciation of force, but a deeper dedication to minimizing its place in human life.

Postscripts to the
Second Edition

POSTSCRIPT I

The Death Penalty Debate Revisited

When I wrote the original version of this book in 1985–1986, public opinion polls indicated that a large majority of Americans supported the death penalty. In the years since then, the death penalty seems to have become even more deeply entrenched in U.S. law and society. The Supreme Court, once a source of hope for death penalty opponents, has shown no interest in constitutional challenges to the death penalty. In case after case, the Court majority has seemed most intent on removing obstacles to executions rather than recognizing flaws in the process.

In the arena of electoral politics, opposition to the death penalty all but disappeared in the wake of the 1988 presidential election, in which Democrat Michael Dukakis was badly hurt by his rejection of capital punishment. This was followed by the defeat of Mario Cuomo, another highly visible death penalty opponent, in the 1994 election for governor of New York. Cuomo's successor, George Pataki, moved quickly and successfully to enact a death penalty law in New York. Following these victories for the death penalty and its supporters, few political candidates have been willing to take a public stance against capital punishment. As a presidential candidate, Bill Clinton sought to distance himself and his party from the abolitionist position, and as president, he worked to increase the number of federal crimes punishable by death. During the 2000 presidential election, neither the Democratic (Al Gore) nor the Republican (George W. Bush) presidential candidate opposed the death penalty. While there are some exceptions, most candidates seem to view support for the death penalty as an unofficial qualification for public office in the United States.

The lack of political candidates who oppose the death penalty is unfortunate for two reasons. First, it makes progress toward abolition less likely. Second, since much public debate occurs in the context of political elections, the lack of abolitionist candidates means that the death penalty is not actively debated. It is difficult to have a debate when only one side is represented in the public realm, and it is difficult for political candidates to oppose the death penalty if, as a result, many voters will see them as "soft on crime" or "caring more about criminals than victims."

These facts about public opinion and the behavior of politicians need to be taken seriously. While the death penalty debate involves theoretical and philosophical issues, its ultimate focus is on the policies we actually choose and implement. People who care about reforming actual policies need to take an interest in how issues are understood by the public at large and by public officials.[1]

At the same time, no philosophical examination of the death penalty can accept public opinion or current policies as the last word on its moral legitimacy. Since Socrates, philosophers have often been gadflies and critics, drawing attention to errors and inconsistencies in widely accepted beliefs. No doubt it is discouraging to face a powerful consensus in favor of a policy that one opposes, but such a consensus can also be seen as a challenge to construct criticisms that will weaken support for a mistaken view. Hence the motivation to argue, even when others think that all is settled.

Still, given the facts I have just stated about politics and public opinion, it is easy to think that death penalty opponents are in a weak position—possessing only words to move what appears to be a mountain of support for the death penalty.

Good News for Death Penalty Opponents

This description may in fact be too gloomy. From 1987 to 2001, the percentage of Americans expressing support for the death penalty dropped from about 75 percent to 67 percent.[2] State legislatures in Nebraska and New Hampshire have voted for a death penalty moratorium or abolition (although both were vetoed by governors). After newspaper reports that errors and official misconduct had put innocent people on death row, Republican Governor George Ryan of Illinois imposed a moratorium on executions in Illinois.[3] Even in Texas, the leading death penalty state in recent years, reforms of the death penalty have been implemented following the attention to the Texas system during the 2000 presidential election. Texans were apparently distressed by negative public reactions to the large number of executions, death sentences for mentally retarded defendants, and low quality legal representation for poor defendants who could not hire their own lawyers. Paradoxically, the execution of Timothy McVeigh has brought to the surface many expressions of unease and unhappiness with the death penalty, even though his crime was so ghastly and destructive.

In addition, the persistence of capital punishment in the United States has increasingly stood out as country after country across the world has abolished the death penalty. In 1995, following the end of the apartheid regime in South Africa, the South African Supreme Court ruled the death penalty unconstitutional in that country, and the European Union now requires abolition of the death penalty as a condition for EU membership.[4]

I cite these facts not to predict the demise of the death penalty. The fact that change is possible is meant as encouragement for those who oppose capital punishment, but change by itself does not establish what is right or wrong, just or unjust. The future can contain regress as well as progress.[5] My inquiry is primarily evaluative. It is an attempt to understand whether a world without the death penalty is better than a world with it. In this context, the reasons both for and against the death penalty retain their importance and continue to deserve our attention.

Coming Attractions

In the following sections of this postscript, I will try to deepen the discussion of the death penalty in three ways. First, I will consider whether the death penalty is a "gut issue." No doubt it is in the sense that many people have strong feelings about it. But is it a "gut issue" in the sense that attempts to reason about it are necessarily impotent and irrelevant?

Second, I will consider whether it is possible to construct a "knockdown" argument against the death penalty view. That is, is it possible to construct an argument that is so strong that it will convince any rational person that the death penalty should be abolished? One might think that if conclusive arguments are not possible, then the issue is merely a matter of gut reactions. I will argue against the gut issue conception of the death penalty debate, but I will also explain why we ought not to expect knockdown arguments on matters like this.

Third, and paradoxically (if not foolishly), I will try to construct an argument that is strong enough to be a knockdown argument. The argument that I offer builds on the discussions that formed the original book rather than superceding them. But my hope is that the argument presents the case against the death penalty in a more sharply focused, powerful, and compelling way.

POSTSCRIPT II

Is the Death Penalty a Gut Issue?

Because the death penalty issue arouses such strong feelings, it seems to be a paradigm of the so-called gut issue—the kind of question that is not susceptible to reasoning. Actually, people tend to describe views about the death penalty in two ways, both of which suggest inflexibility of belief and a lack of responsiveness to arguments. For some, the death penalty is a gut issue—a matter of visceral emotional response, while others see it is a matter of conscience, principle, or deep moral conviction. Either way, our guts are not open to argument, and our basic principles are things that we are reluctant to compromise or amend. Neither approach leaves room for serious reasoning or encourages attention to facts about the way that the death penalty actually operates in the real world.

The gut issue view of the disagreement about the death penalty is vividly captured in the language of South African Supreme Court Justice Albie Sachs. He writes:

Decent people throughout the world are divided over which arouses the greatest horror: the thought of the State deliberately killing its citizens, or the idea of allowing cruel killers to co-exist with honest citizens.[6]

Sachs's reference to the "horror" felt by people conveys the emotional power of the death penalty issue. His focus on the fact that these opposing horrors are felt by "decent people" on both sides suggests that we cannot simply dismiss everyone on the side we oppose as moral barbarians. If decent people disagree and do so with horror—not mildly and not with a recognition that something can be said for the other side—then perhaps trying to reason won't get us very far.

Doubts about the Gut Issue Model

Apt as this description seems, I want to argue against its accuracy. I do so because the way we classify an issue can shape our response to it, and the gut issue image is a powerful obstacle to reasoned debate. There are several reasons why we should resist accepting it. First, calling something a "gut issue" may itself be a useful rationalization or a tactic for people who have neither facts nor logical arguments on their side. Because the "gut issue" label can deflect attention from their inability to defend their view, we should not automatically accept it on any important question.

Second, calling something a "gut issue" can be a self-fulfilling prophecy. If we all agree that rational discussion about an issue is impossible, we will not even try to reason about it. Nor will we try to understand the beliefs of our opponents or look for common ground that might diminish or resolve our disagreements. It will become a matter of visceral response because we have refused to approach it with our minds.

Finally, this classification has implications for other issues. If the death penalty were the only issue about which decent people passionately disagreed, we might be forced to live with the "gut issue" label in this case. But there are many such issues, and they are often matters of great importance. To classify them all as beyond reasonable discussion is to forsake reason as a means of dealing with moral, political, and social conflict. The philosopher Karl Popper once wrote that the rejection of reasoning "must lead to an appeal to violence and brutal force as the ultimate arbiter in any dispute."[7] While this may be an overstatement, Popper certainly has a point. If we want to avoid violence and brute force, we must make the effort to discuss issues about which there is passionate disagreement. We need to learn how to disagree in productive, respectful ways, how to seek resolutions, and how to narrow our differences.

These are all reasons for hoping that the "gut issue" image is false, but to show it is false requires some evidence. In what follows, I will consider three types of evidence against the "gut issue" image. I want to show that reasoning about the death penalty occurs and has an impact on people's beliefs. The fact that these beliefs are passionately held is quite compatible with reason playing an important role in shaping them.

Historical Evidence

The history of crimes and punishments over the last several hundred years is a complex process with multiple causes. Nonetheless, I suggest that we can see the changing history of the death penalty during the last three hundred years as a kind of prolonged social negotiation process. At the start, many more crimes were punishable by death. For example, more than two hundred crimes were punishable by death in England by the early 1800s. In colonial America, a wide variety of crimes were punishable by death, not only murder but also rape, robbery, sodomy, counterfeiting, and horse theft. Daniell Frank, the first person executed in the American colonies, was hanged for stealing a calf. Often, death was the mandatory punishment and executions were carried out as public spectacles. Legal safeguards for defendants were limited, and death was frequently imposed in gruesome, painful ways. In 1812, an English judge sentenced members of a group guilty of treason to be hanged, but not until death; after being taken down from the gallows alive, the prisoners were to have their bowels cut out and burned before their eyes. Finally, they were to be beheaded and their bodies cut in quarters.[8]

Opposition to the death penalty arose in both England and the United States in the late eighteenth and early nineteenth centuries. In the United States, the death penalty was abolished in sixteen states between 1846 and 1917 and in eleven more from 1957 to 1972.[9] Even in states where abolition efforts failed, significant

changes occurred. The number of crimes punishabl
was restricted, and executions for specific crimes were
cretionary rather than mandatory. Executions were tra..siormed
from public displays to private events, while the means of execution were altered in a quest to make them more humane—from
hanging to the electric chair, the gas chamber, and lethal injection. Guarantees of legal representation and elaborate procedures
governing trials and sentences were written into law.

In describing this process of reform, I do not mean to suggest
that the death penalty is now humane, just, or morally acceptable. Nor do I mean that there has been steady progress away from
the death penalty. Since the 1960s we have seen increased public
support for the death penalty, and after a brief period when the
Supreme Court invalidated existing death penalty laws, the death
penalty returned with a vengeance. The number of executions
has risen in recent years and the number of people on death row
has increased. Nonetheless, some objectionable features have
been diminished, and, I suggest, we can see these changes as
resulting *in part* from a long process of public reasoning. The fact
that the death penalty has survived does not show that its supporters were completely unresponsive to the criticisms of abolitionists. While remaining unconvinced by the abolitionist
position, they sometimes came to see aspects of the death penalty
process as unjust and inhumane, and they tried to alter the process to make it consistent with their values.

Over time, the issues become narrowed, making the remaining
issues more difficult to resolve and lending credence to the view
that reasoning does not matter. The history that got us to this
point, however, strongly suggests that a social reasoning process—what Amitai Etzioni calls a "megalogue" or societywide dia-
logue—has been going on and has brought about real changes.[10]
The process is by no means smooth or continuous, and it is often
influenced by misconceptions about crime, criminals, and the
legal process. Nonetheless, changes in the practice of capital punishment can be seen as evidence of a process of social debate
rather than evidence of the impotence of reasoning.

While I offer this history as evidence for a process of public
reasoning, I grant that the evidence is far from conclusive. Advocates of the gut issue view could describe these changes as the
result of shifts in feeling and sentiment rather than shifts in

belief. That hypothesis is compatible with the historical facts I have cited, but so is the hypothesis of reason-driven change that I have suggested. While it may be hard to see how one could prove that these changes resulted from rational argument, it is no less hard to see how a defender of the gut issue perspective could show that all of these changes resulted from shifting emotions and that reason and evidence played no role in the process.

The moral of the story may be that it is foolish to look either to reason or passion as the sole cause of change. It is much more plausible that both have played a role. While the "gut issue" label presupposes an all-or-nothing perspective—either all reason or all passion—it is hard to believe that the changes over time occurred simply because of one cause or the other. Advocates of rational debate can acknowledge that feelings play an important role while insisting that even strong feelings about issues can be influenced by fact and argument. It is advocates of the gut issue perspective who must defend the implausible view that reasons have played no role at all.

Once we acknowledge the role of both reasons and passions in the process of historical change, it becomes clear that it is foolish to distinguish so sharply between gut issues—about which passions alone call the shots—and rational disagreements, about which we decide purely on the basis of logic and empirical evidence. In fact, nonrational factors play a role even in factual, scientific debates, and reasons can influence our feelings.[11] While advocates of rational debate can acknowledge both rational and passional sources of belief, those who invoke the concept of a gut issue to stifle debate are committed to an implausible either/or model.

The Difficulties of Knowing What We Believe

I draw a second form of evidence against the "gut issue" model from my experience teaching courses on controversial moral and political issues. I have found that people often misdescribe their own beliefs and that their descriptions often make them sound more absolutist and inflexible than they really are. Hearing their descriptions, we are likely to decide that because people's beliefs are unshakeable and unrevisable, there is no possibility of reasoning with them. But if people's beliefs are less absolutist than their self-descriptions suggest, they may be more open to reasoned argument than their descriptions lead us to believe.

To illustrate how people misdescribe their own beliefs, I will give an example that involves an issue other than the death penalty: gun control. My contention is that in this case, people's beliefs about their beliefs are often mistaken and that the result of this misunderstanding is a misleading, overly polarized image of the debate on this issue.

In my experience, people who oppose gun control often say that they believe in an absolute right to defend oneself and others from violent attack. Based on this right, they claim that individuals have an absolute right to own weapons and that governments have no right to restrict the possession of weapons. Frequently they cite the Second Amendment's reference to the right "to bear arms" as a constitutional guarantor of their position. These assertions are often expressed with great passion, and contrary assertions in favor of restrictions on these (alleged) rights are viewed with the same sort of horror that Albie Sachs spoke of in connection with the death penalty. In addition, people with these views sometimes see governments as untrustworthy, and they fear that without a right to own weapons, citizens will be at the mercy of governments that have gone astray.

People with these views often say that they oppose all forms of gun control. At the same time, I have found that some people who say these things do not actually believe them. In fact, without much effort, one can show that they reject an absolute right to own weapons and accept the need for government to play a role in limiting access to them. In particular, they generally accept two sorts of restrictions on the right to own weapons:

1. limits on the *kinds of weapons* that individuals have a right to own, and
2. limits on *what types of people* should be able to own weapons.

Regarding limits on the kinds of weapons, self-described defenders of unrestricted rights to own weapons will readily agree that the right of individual citizens to own and "bear arms" does not extend to ownership of "arms" such as nuclear weapons, tanks, bombs, or artillery. Regarding limits on which people may own weapons, they are often adamant that both individuals with criminal records and people who are mentally ill have no right to own weapons.

These views are clearly incompatible with their initial stated opinion that individuals have an absolute right to own weapons to defend themselves. Moreover, while their stated view is that governments cannot be trusted with the power to restrict ownership of weapons, any policy that prohibits people with criminal records or mental illness from owning weapons requires government officials to determine who belongs to these groups. Likewise, decisions about which weapons are too dangerous to be owned by individuals must be made by legislative bodies, and laws forbidding access to such weapons must be enforced by the police and the courts. Any restrictions require that government officials have the authority to enforce them.

I am not saying that everyone would accept these restrictions or that there is no disagreement on gun control. The people I am describing accept these restrictions but still disagree strongly with those who seek to ban gun ownership by private citizens. Nonetheless, there is a middle ground that many people on both sides accept. Middle grounds are often disliked, however, because they do not conform to anyone's ideals.

Why people misunderstand their own views is an interesting question. Why do we characterize our beliefs in absolutist terms while at the same time affirm restrictions that are incompatible with these absolutist views? It may be that advocates for particular causes find it easier to rally support for categorical positions than for complex views that contain qualifications. Complex views are harder to state in brief, memorable sound bites and harder to fit on banners and bumper stickers. In addition, advocates may find it strategically valuable to voice their positions as if they were nonnegotiable. Finally, people on all parts of the moral/political spectrum often see adherence to principled, uncompromising positions as a virtue. Contrasted with unprincipled opportunism, principled stands look quite attractive, but we pay a price for this model of moral integrity. It often impedes reasoned debate, blocks efforts to understand the complexity of issues, and produces intolerance and animosity toward people with opposing views.

Drawing on my teaching experience, then, I want to suggest

that the descriptions that we initially give of our views are often misleading oversimplifications. If we want to find out what people believe about an issue, we have to question them at length, not only so that we can get more information from them but also—and perhaps more importantly—because they need to figure out what their views actually are. My anecdotal evidence for these claims receives support from a study by Phoebe Ellsworth and Samuel Gross. They write:

> Except for radical conversion experiences, people are rarely aware that their attitudes have changed: they report their current attitudes as attitudes they have held as long as they can remember. Similarly, most people are unable to give an accurate account of the reasons for their attitudes.[12]

Misconceptions about our own beliefs, then, are not uncommon and are well known to scholars of public opinion.

Since ordinary life may not offer the need or opportunity to articulate our views, it is important to create circumstances in which this kind of reflection goes on. The possibility of reasoned debate increases when people become aware of the complexity of both their own opinions and the issues that we face together. This awareness may be in short supply, however, when issues are emotionally charged and when uncompromising stands are socially encouraged.

Evidence from Public Opinion Polls

Contrary to popular opinion, evidence from public opinion polls shows that people's beliefs about the death penalty are more complex than they appear and that people are less supportive of capital punishment than many have claimed. Public opinion polls have both created and reinforced an oversimplified perspective because they limit themselves to asking people one simple question. When polls go beyond these simple questions, they reveal forms of complexity and implicit reasoning that are less enthusiastic about the death penalty and that do not conform to the "gut issue" model.

Consider the following Gallup poll figures.[13] During the period of August 29 to September 5, 2000, Gallup asked people what is called the SPQ, or standard polling question: "Are you in favor of the death penalty for a person convicted of murder?'' This question drew the following distribution of responses: favor the death penalty: 67 percent; oppose the death penalty, 28 percent; no opinion, 5 percent.

The same poll then asked: "If you could choose between the following two approaches, which do you think is the better penalty for murder: the death penalty or life imprisonment, with absolutely no possibility of parole?" This question drew the following response: favor the death penalty, 49 percent; favor life imprisonment without parole, 47 percent; no opinion, 4 percent.

The different responses to these inquiries raise a number of questions about what people actually believe. Do 67 percent favor the death penalty? Or is it 49 percent? And how should we describe the views of the 18 percent of people who answered the first question by saying they favored the death penalty and then answered the second question by saying that if they could, they would choose life imprisonment without parole rather than the death penalty? What exactly do they believe? Are they for or against?[14]

I draw three conclusions from these data and the shifts they reveal.

Defects of the Standard Polling Question

First, question number 1—the standard polling question—is badly defective. This is important because reports of responses to question number 1 have profoundly shaped our view of public opinion about the death penalty.[15] It is these reports that have created the impression of overwhelming public support for capital punishment. Question number 1 is defective because it simply asks people whether they favor or oppose the death penalty. In matters of public policy, however, what we favor or oppose often depends on the alternatives that are available to us. When people answer question number 1, they may either be ignoring relevant options, or their answers may be based on implicit comparisons that the survey does not reveal. In either case, making the alternatives explicit will affect people's expressed beliefs about the legitimacy of capital punishment. Since question number 1 does not make alternatives explicit, it does not reveal people's beliefs in an unambiguous way.

If we take seriously the idea that people's responses are affected by the alternatives offered, then it becomes clear that it is inaccurate to say simply that people are for or against the death penalty. Except for people who favor or oppose the death penalty no matter what, an accurate description would have to say that they favor the death penalty over some alternatives and oppose it by comparison to others. This is why question number 2 is superior to number 1. Question number 2 provides a gauge of opinion in the context of an explicit comparison between the death penalty and one plausible alternative to it.

Even question number 2, however, does not give us a full picture. Suppose that we asked those who support the death penalty (rather than life imprisonment without parole) whether they would support this option if they believed that there was: (a) almost no chance of executing innocent people, or (b) a substantial probability that innocent people would be executed. It is certainly conceivable that some people would accept the death penalty under condition (a) but not under condition (b). Question number 2 alone would not reveal that difference.

This is important because confidence in the reliability of our system for identifying guilty people may be an important factor for some people; a loss of confidence in the system might move them to oppose the death penalty, even though they would support it under other circumstances. Similarly, some people who prefer life imprisonment without parole might do so because they do not trust the system. With greater confidence in the system's reliability, they might support the death penalty instead of life without parole. These important features of people's beliefs are not captured either by the single standard polling questions or by question number 2.

Polls As Evidence of Reasoning

My second conclusion from the poll data is that the combination of the two sets of questions and answers provides evidence of certain forms of reasoning—at least for some of the people sampled. As we have seen, the Gallup poll shows that support for the death penalty drops from 67 percent to 49 percent when people are offered the alternative of life imprisonment without parole.

While many continued to favor the death penalty, 18 percent—which is more than one quarter of those who initially said they favor the death penalty—shifted their view. For these people, the death penalty does not appear to be a gut issue, since offering a satisfactory alternative seems to trigger a form of comparative reasoning that leads to a change of position.

The poll results do not tell us, of course, what this reasoning is, but a plausible interpretation is suggested by William Bowers.[16] In surveys of both ordinary citizens and jurors in death penalty cases, Bowers found that people's beliefs about the death penalty are influenced by their beliefs about the length of prison sentences for people convicted of murder, and their desire to prevent murderers from killing again. If people believe that imprisonment will keep convicted murderers from ever threatening the lives of other people, then they are less likely to support the death penalty. By contrast, if they believe that convicted murderers will serve relatively short sentences and once again endanger the lives of others, then they are more likely to support the death penalty.

According to Bowers, many people care about what is called the "incapacitation" function of punishment; they want to make sure that murderers will never again pose a threat to the lives of others. As a result, their view about the death penalty is influenced by their beliefs about whether alternatives to the death penalty achieve—or fail to achieve—the goal of incapacitation. In addition, he argues, many of those who care about incapacitation support the death penalty because they do not believe that the alternatives achieve the goal of incapacitation. Their beliefs about this failure, however, rest on misconceptions about the amount of time that convicted murderers actually spend in prison.

Table 1 shows the results of 1991 surveys in New York and Nebraska. It compares people's beliefs about prison sentences for murder with actual sentences for murder in those states. As it shows, many people seriously underestimate the amount of time that convicted murderers spend in prison.

As Table 1 shows, roughly half the respondents in both New York and Nebraska hold the false belief that convicted murderers would be paroled or released within fifteen years. Indeed, 20 to 25 percent thought that convicted murderers would serve less than ten years. The facts are quite different. In New York state at the time of the study, the law required a mandatory minimum of

TABLE 1

	New York	Nebraska
percent who believe that murderers serve *less than* 10 years	25.6	20.4
percent who believe that murderers serve *10–15* years	29.6	27.9
percent who believe that murderers serve *less than 15* years	55.2	48.3
Legally required punishment for first-degree murder	Mandatory minimum: 15 years before consideration of parole	Mandatory life imprisonment without parole

fifteen years for people convicted of first-degree murder before they could even be considered for parole. Nebraska's law was much more stringent, requiring life imprisonment without parole for any murder for which death is a possible punishment.[17] Yet almost half the people in Nebraska believed that their state punished convicted murderers relatively leniently.

According to Bowers, these false beliefs lead many people to conclude that "the currently available alternatives [to the death penalty] are insufficiently harsh or meaningful."[18] If they had accurate knowledge about sentences for murder, this might lead them to alter their beliefs. If they knew the actual prison sentences for murder, they would see that the sentences satisfy their desire to insure that murderers will not kill again.

Bowers's research also indicates that death penalty support can be diminished by creating attractive alternatives to the death penalty. As evidence for this conclusion, Bowers cites surveys in which people were asked two questions. First, they were simply asked whether they supported the death penalty; then they were asked the following question:

> Suppose convicted first-degree murderers in this state could be sentenced to *life in prison without parole* and also be required to *work in prison for money that would go to the families of their victims.* Would you prefer this as an alternative to the death penalty? (emphasis added)[19]

When restitution to victims' families was added to life imprisonment without parole, support for the death penalty dropped con-
siderably.

As Table 2 shows, when people were simply asked if they favor
or oppose the death penalty, the results seem to indicate overwhelming support for the death penalty:

In every state, more than 70 percent of respondents indicated
support for the death penalty. When they were offered the alternative of life imprisonment without parole and restitution to victims' families, however, their stated preferences shifted
dramatically away from the death penalty.

As Table 3 shows, in every state sampled, a majority would
oppose the death penalty if there were an alternative to it that
they regarded as suitable and attractive.

Bowers's work is instructive in a number of ways. First, his survey results cast doubt on the almost universal view that people
overwhelmingly support the death penalty. Second, his research,
comparing actual prison terms for convicted murderers with
beliefs about prison terms, makes clear the public's ignorance on
these issues and the effects of this ignorance on people's views.
Finally, by showing how support for the death penalty is related
to views about the goals of punishment and beliefs about current
policies, Bowers's claims lend support to the view that people's
beliefs about the death penalty are not simply gut responses but
are based in part on forms of reasoning and factual assumptions.

An Alternative View?

A different picture of the dynamics of public opinion is drawn
by Phoebe Ellsworth and Samuel Gross. Their view seems to run
counter to the rational image suggested by Bowers's studies. They
see people as less interested in alternatives to the death penalty
and less reasoned in their approach to the death penalty than

TABLE 2

	Favor death penalty	Oppose death penalty	Not sure	Poll date
Florida	84.0	13.0	3.0	May 1986
Georgia	75.0	25.0	—	June 1986
California	79.5	19.0	—	December 1989
New York	70.6	21.8	8.0	March 1991
Nebraska	80.4	13.4	6.1	April 1991

Bowers's claims suggest. In this way, their view lends support to the "gut image" model.

Ellsworth and Gross see support for the death penalty as related to what they call people's "ideological self-definition." When people have an intense belief or commitment to certain values, they think of themselves as constituted in part by these values. The values become parts of their sense of self-identity. If support for or opposition to the death penalty come to form a part of their conception of themselves, then these beliefs will acquire a certain stability. Because people's "self-definition" is unlikely to change rapidly, it follows that if their beliefs about the death penalty become part of their sense of self, then those beliefs will be less likely to change in response to arguments and debates.[20]

One reason why Ellsworth and Gross reject a more rationalistic image of public opinion is that, as they put it, most Americans "care a great deal about the death penalty but know little about it, and have no particular desire to know."[21] Nonetheless, Ellsworth and Gross note a relationship between support for the death penalty and people's beliefs about the extent of crime. Support for the death penalty rose in the late '60s and '70s as people became increasingly aware of and concerned about rising crime. The more that death penalty attitudes are related to beliefs about factual matters, the more they are potentially open to influence by reason. But if such beliefs depend primarily on stable features of people's identity, then these beliefs will be more fixed and less capable of influence by reason.

Having It Both Ways

Each of these conceptions of the dynamics of public opinion sounds plausible, and yet they also seem to contradict one

TABLE 3

	Prefer life + restitution	*Prefer death penalty*	*Undecided/ No opinion*	*Poll Date*
Florida	70	24	6	May 1986
Georgia	51	43	5	December 1986
California	67	26	7	December 1989
New York	73	19	8	March 1991
Nebraska	64	26	10	April 1991

another. As a defender of the relevance of rational arguments, I naturally find Bowers's studies both illuminating and encouraging. Since so much has been made of the apparent consensus in favor of the death penalty and the apparent rigidity of people's views, it is encouraging to find evidence against this bleak vision. Even if we allow for a certain amount of "belief inertia," that is, for a natural human reluctance to change important beliefs, both Bowers's research and the Gallup poll data cast doubt on the somewhat inflexible image suggested by Ellsworth and Gross.[22]

It may be, however, that we do not have to choose between these two conceptions. After all, when we speak of public opinion, we are talking about the beliefs of many different people, and the intensity of belief or disbelief in the death penalty will vary among them, as will the causal origins of their views. It is certainly not part of my view that everyone's opinions are flexible and responsive to reason. Nor does Bowers assert that death penalty support derives entirely from misconceptions about current sentences and concerns about incapacitation. Ellsworth and Gross are undoubtedly right that for some people, their sense of self may be so deeply entwined with their views on the death penalty or other similarly charged issues that change of belief is only as likely as change of self. But presumably this is not true for everyone with an opinion about the death penalty.

From the perspective of public policy, what is important is whether flexibility in belief and openness to evidence are rare phenomena or whether they are widespread enough to make change possible. In a later work, Ellsworth and Gross suggest the ways in which social conditions can alter people's receptiveness to change of belief.[23] Events in the wider world may make people more resistant to change of belief at some times and less resistant at others.

Again, the error would seem to be the adoption of an either/or view. As I argued earlier, defenders of the role of reason do not need to hold an overly rationalistic view of the dynamics of belief and belief change. I have stressed evidence of the role of reason because people are often skeptical about the power of argument in this area. Once this role is acknowledged, however, there is no reason to deny the impact of other kinds of factors. Since the death penalty engages both our reason and our passions, where we stand will be influenced by both.

Misconceptions about Death Penalty Opposition

Before concluding this part of the discussion, I want to make clear that the points I have made about the character of beliefs apply as much to death penalty opponents as supporters. I believe that death penalty opponents often misunderstand and misrepresent their beliefs, just as death penalty supporters do. Likewise, death penalty opponents are often unaware of factual assumptions that are presupposed by what they would describe as absolute principles.

Consider the first point: misrepresenting beliefs. Death penalty opponents often say that they reject capital punishment because they think it is simply wrong for the state to take human lives. Yet this cannot be what most of them actually believe. These same people usually think that police officers are sometimes justified in using deadly force to ward off threats to themselves or others. Likewise, many death penalty opponents believe that it is some-times morally permissible for countries to go to war. Anyone who thinks that these activities can be justified cannot be committed to the view that the state ought never to engage in killing.[24]

What about the role of factual assumptions? While many people seem to oppose the death penalty in an absolute, principled way, I suspect that there are circumstances in which they would support it. If this is true, then their opposition rests not just on principles but also on assumptions about facts. To see this, consider two hypothetical cases, one completely fantastic, the other apparently more realistic

Here is the fantastic case: suppose that executing a murderer had the effect of restoring the life of that murderer's victim(s). If capital punishment had this effect, it would certainly be attractive in a number of ways. Since the victim was unjustly deprived of life and since killing the murderer to prevent him or her from killing the victim would have been justifiable self-defense or defense of others, it is hard to see why killing the murderer to restore the victim to life would be less justified. While there are complications even in this case, I have no doubt that many people who oppose the death penalty would support it if the facts matched this fantasy.[25]

Or suppose, again hypothetically and contrary to the actual facts, that the death penalty had extremely powerful deterrent effects. Suppose that small numbers of executions deterred vast numbers of homicides and that no other punishment had such deterrent power. Suppose, too, that no other social or legal policy had similar effects—that ending poverty, prohibiting gun ownership, and banning violent entertainment had been tried and had failed to diminish homicides. If this were so, it would be much harder to oppose the death penalty. There would still be serious problems about arbitrariness, discrimination, and the possibility of executing innocent people. There would still be a need for legal safeguards to ensure procedural justice. But under these conditions, death penalty supporters could claim that, on balance, the death penalty provides the best means to honor and protect human life.

Of course, all of this is a fantasy too. States and countries without the death penalty are generally safer than those that have it, and responsible advocates of the death penalty make no large claims about deterrence because they know there is no evidence for them. My point, however, is that when death penalty opponents express their views as categorical principles, they are assuming that the facts are not as I have imagined them. In rejecting the death penalty, they are implicitly assuming that it neither restores victims to life nor makes a serious difference in homicide rates. If it did either of these, death penalty opponents would face a more complex and difficult moral choice.

I would argue, then, that death penalty opponents are as likely to misunderstand their beliefs as death penalty advocates. For most people, these beliefs are unlikely to be as categorical as they are often made out to be. They appear categorical because people assume a certain factual context and within that context think it self-evident that we either ought to impose capital punishment or ought not to do so. Part of the work of clarifying the death penalty issue involves bringing to the surface the various presuppositions—both moral and factual—that shape our beliefs, and seeing whether these beliefs are warranted. Since many of these beliefs are factual, any serious examination of the death penalty must pay attention to factual matters. There cannot be a purely abstract, philosophical solution to the problem of capital punishment.[26]

POSTSCRIPT III

Can There Be a Knockdown Argument against the Death Penalty?

Approaching this question, I am drawn in two opposing directions. As an advocate, I would like to believe that if I were skillful enough, I could make such a strong case against the death penalty that it would constitute a "knockdown" argument. (This is what I tried to do in the original version of this book, and in the final part of this postscript, I will try again.) At the same time, reflection on the nature of the debate leads me to think we should not expect knockdown arguments on such issues as the death penalty.

Of course, people who think the death penalty is a gut issue will agree that there cannot be knockdown arguments about it, but they do so because they see the question as purely emotional. My reasons are different. The death penalty debate involves complex, open-ended sets of moral and factual beliefs, and this feature makes it unrealistic to think that they can be easily settled by relevant arguments. In this section, I want to show how we can acknowledge this fact without forsaking a belief in the relevance of rational argument to this sort of issue.

First, then, what are "knockdown" arguments and why should we not expect them on this type of question? The idea of a knockdown argument has two parts. The first derives from a model of reasoning that is influential both in philosophy and in ordinary life. According to this model, if an issue is susceptible to reasoning, it must be possible to construct arguments that would convince any rational person of the truth or falsity of one of the opposing views. A knockdown argument has this property: It *would convince any rational person.* I will call this *the conclusive reason postulate.* The second part of the idea of a knockdown argument is psychological. I will call it the *postulate of instantaneous results.* It tests to see whether an argument is conclusive by seeing if it can cause a change in belief as soon as it is understood.

Descartes conveys these ideas in his *Rules for the Direction of the Mind.* He writes:

> [W]henever two men come to opposite decisions about the same matter one of them at least must certainly be in the wrong, and

apparently there is not even one of them who knows [the truth]; for if the reasoning of the second was sound and clear, he would be able so to lay it before the other as finally to succeed in convincing *his* understanding also.[27]

According to Descartes, real knowledge is only possible when we have knockdown arguments, "sound and clear" arguments that actually convince people. If such arguments are lacking, then there is no real knowledge, and the issue at hand cannot be settled by rational means.

This model of reasoning reinforces the notion that reason can play no role in questions on such issues as the death penalty.[28] Single arguments almost never have the power that the conclusive reason postulate requires, and people seldom change their views on important or complicated questions in the way that the instantaneous result postulate requires. If reasoning is only efficacious under these conditions, then it is not efficacious on any controversial issue.

Problems with the Conclusive Reason Postulate

Neither of these postulates is reasonable to accept, however. The conclusive reason postulate works only in areas where we can offer proofs, because the set of relevant considerations is very limited. This is true in fields like geometry or logic. In these contexts, a single argument that draws on the relevant considerations in the proper way can conclusively establish a particular conclusion. It is also true in some practical contexts when the parameters of a decision have already been set. If I absolutely need a car, have limited funds, and find that there is only one car for sale that I can afford, then there is a conclusive reason for me to buy it.

The death penalty debate differs from both of these cases because many different types of considerations are relevant to it. To see this, consider death penalty supporters who defend it by saying that it deters homicides better than other punishments. In response, death penalty opponents can appeal to the studies like those cited in chapter 2, which show that there is no good evidence that the death penalty deters homicide better than long-term imprisonment.[29]

Suppose that the death penalty supporter examines the empirical evidence and concedes that the death penalty is not a superior deterrent. Must this person cease to support the death penalty? Is this a knockdown argument? The answer depends on whether the person's support for the death penalty was based solely on concerns about deterrence. If it was, then reason would require that person to forsake the death penalty.

For most people, however, their support for (or opposition to) the death penalty does not rest on a single basis. Most people's views are based on multiple reasons. If one basis is refuted, they will appeal to others in order to maintain their belief. They will say that the death penalty is still justified because it is what murderers deserve, or it is the best way to show respect for murder victims, or it is less costly than life imprisonment. Indeed, they may say all of these things and others as well. Because there are multiple bases of belief, no *single* argument can be a knockdown argument. Even if it conclusively refutes one of the arguments on which the belief rests, other arguments remain to provide support for it.

The defender of knockdown arguments can try to salvage the idea in the following way. If we view a series of related arguments as the components of a single, multipart argument, then we may still think it possible to have conclusive arguments about issues like the death penalty. While no single (part of the) argument can be a knockdown argument by itself, a combination of arguments might achieve this status. The structure of my argument in the original version of this book matches this description. I tried to raise every major value that death penalty supporters might appeal to—respect for life, deterrence, what punishment is deserved, vengeance, and symbolic expressiveness—and in each case, I tried to refute the argument appealing to that value. In addition, I presented several positive reasons against the death penalty—its arbitrary and discriminatory imposition, its being cruel and unusual because it is unnecessary for either deterrence or retribution, and the risk of executing innocent people. My hope was that the combination of positive and negative arguments would form a conclusive refutation of the position to support the death penalty and a conclusive defense of the position to oppose the death penalty. If it succeeded, it would meet the conclusive reason postulate.

Psychological Barriers to Receptiveness

Even if I had succeeded in creating the best possible arguments, it would be foolish to think that I had produced a knockdown argument. This pessimistic—but nonetheless realistic—attitude arises from the following fact: whether an argument is a knockdown argument depends not only on the *logical* features of the argument itself but also on the *psychological* features of the people to whom it is addressed. Even the best of arguments may be psychologically ineffective, not because they are logically weak but because psychological barriers prevent people from responding to the argument's force.

Why might people fail to respond to good arguments? First, people—all of us—are resistant to changing beliefs that are important or that we have held with a high degree of conviction. Second, even if death penalty supporters could not answer the arguments I gave, they might explain this as a lack of skill on their part. We frequently confront arguments against things we believe and find that we cannot come up with good objections to them. But our inability at that time does not mean that we will be unable to think of arguments later. Or, even if we personally cannot show why an argument is defective, we may think that someone smarter or more skillful in debate might be able to do so. Third, as the complexity of an argument increases, its psychological impact may decrease because it makes greater demands on our attention. As David Hume noted long ago:

> [T]he conviction which arises from a subtle reasoning diminishes in proportion to the efforts, which the imagination makes to enter into the reasoning, and to conceive it in all its parts.[30]

A one-page argument that is easy to comprehend may pack more psychological wallop than a complex, multipart argument that requires 148 pages of text. But short and sweet arguments are not available on complicated issues. Only complex arguments will do, and what complex arguments gain in completeness may be offset by losses in immediate psychological impact.

Finally, in order for a multipart argument like the one in this book to change someone's mind, it is not enough for that person to consider every argument and think: "Oh, this refutes one of the bases of my support for the death penalty." Rather, to be con-

vinced, a person must go through something like the following
set of thoughts:

1. I support the death penalty for reasons A, B, and C.
2. This part of the book refutes reason A; another part refutes
   reason B; and a third part refutes reason C.
3. I do not think that these refutations are mistaken.
4. Nor do I have other reasons to support my position.
5. The basis of my support for the death penalty has been
   refuted.
6. Therefore, I ought to change my mind and oppose the death
   penalty.

Only after accepting this whole set of beliefs would a person
accept that he or she had encountered a conclusive argument.

The complexity of this response is a powerful reason for not
being too optimistic about the power of arguments. Not only does
it require someone to understand and evaluate the results of several arguments together; it also requires them to have a high level
of confidence in their own reasoning ability. If people have been
brought up to believe something on authority or if most people
that they know share their belief, then having these thoughts will
require them to pit their own judgment against the collective
beliefs of others whom they admire or respect. People who are
unsure of themselves will not take this step.

In addition, there can be social and emotional pressures against
changing a belief. Patrick Reeder, whose wife died in the Oklahoma City bombing, moved from strongly desiring the execution
of Timothy McVeigh to opposing it. In making this move, he had
to overcome strong social pressures. According to journalist Jeff
Goodell:

> Reeder understood that to oppose the execution meant not only
> alienating friends and family who, like him, were deeply dam-
> aged by Mr. McVeigh. It meant challenging the bedrock values
> of the place he lives. It meant having his love of his wife ques-
> tioned. It meant cold looks at the bank, anonymous phone calls,
> further isolation. He wasn't sure he had the emotional strength
> for it.[31]

While most of us may not face such intense pressures, we may
be wary of opposing views that are dominant among our family,
friends, and colleagues. Social pressures can create strong disin-

centives that can make people reluctant to change widespread beliefs or even to consider that such beliefs might be false. In such cases, it is not our gut response that precludes rational consideration; it is our fear of other people's disapproval and the consequences of that disapproval in our daily lives.

For all these reasons, it is foolish to expect that either single arguments or sets of arguments—even if they are very strong—will invariably succeed in changing people's minds. This is not to say that they will necessarily fail. Some people may be convinced, and others who don't hold a firm opinion may be especially open to the force of reasons. But we ought not to expect even the best arguments to convince everyone.[32]

Even when they fail to convince, however, reasons and arguments may still be efficacious in other ways. They may make people less confident in their belief, less likely to support it publicly, and perhaps more receptive to further negative arguments. Arguments and reasons may lead to support for measures that restrict the death penalty or require stronger procedural safeguards for defendants. They may lead to support for a moratorium on executions. These would be signs of weakened belief, and such weakening can occur even when arguments are not decisively rejected.[33]

There are good reasons, then, to keep raising arguments about these matters, even if we should not be overoptimistic about scoring a knockout.

POSTSCRIPT IV

A Final Try: Why Death Penalty Supporters Ought to Abandon Their Position

Having argued against both excessive optimism and excessive pessimism regarding the power of rational argument, I now want to address death penalty supporters and give them the strongest reasons I can for opposing the death penalty. In framing this argument, I will try to maximize both its logical and its psychological force.

One reason for optimism about this argument is that the death penalty debate differs from some other disagreements in an important way. In some cases, resolving disagreements is hard because people on opposing sides differ in their fundamental values. This makes it difficult to find values that are accepted by both sides and that can serve as a basis for constructing arguments. The death penalty debate is not like this. People who favor the death penalty and people who oppose it often appeal to the same fundamental values: respect for human life and justice.

If we could show that one view about the death penalty is inconsistent with these two values, we would also show that people on that side of the issue are actually contradicting their own deepest values. The strength of this kind of argument is both logical and psychological. It is logically strong because a contradiction is necessarily false; a person holding contradictory views has an overall belief that is necessarily false. It is psychologically strong for two reasons: the form of argument is relatively simple, and the argument appeals only to values that people themselves accept.

Here is the overall structure of the argument that I will now address to death penalty supporters:

1. You accept justice and respect for human life as fundamental values.
2. The death penalty is inconsistent with these values.
3. Therefore, based on your own values, you ought to reject the death penalty.

While it is possible that someone might reject the two values that I appeal to, there would be a great cost to doing so. First, they would deprive themselves of some of the common arguments for capital punishment. Second, they would no longer be seen as having a respectable position in this debate.

Rejecting justice would undermine their status in the debate because society is publicly committed to achieving justice (whether or not it actually takes the required steps to do this). Publicly disavowing justice would show the person to be morally bankrupt and not worthy of being taken seriously. In addition, embracing injustice would undermine death penalty supporters' ability to appeal to such ideas as "an eye for an eye," since that saying derives its force a conception of justice as reciprocity. While I tried to show in chapter 6 that "an eye for an eye" is a defective principle of justice, those who invoke it are at least trying to show that the death penalty is just.

Rejecting respect for the value of human life would have these same two effects. People who do not claim to value life would not be seen as respectable parties to the debate; they would lack any moral credibility. In addition, this rejection would make death penalty advocates' position incoherent. If human life is not important, then murder is not a serious crime, and if murder is not a serious crime, there is no reason to punish it severely. So rejecting the value of human life would make advocacy of the death penalty entirely incomprehensible.

I assume, then, that all who support the death penalty and whose moral views we take seriously are committed to the values of justice and respect for human life. My task, then, is to show that the death penalty is inconsistent with these values. How can this be done?

The Death Penalty in Theory

The first thing to note is that it probably cannot be done if we see the claim that "the death penalty is inconsistent with valuing human life and justice" as a kind of necessary truth. Why is this? Because if we think of the death penalty as an abstraction or Platonic form, then it may be possible to conceive of it in a way that is consistent with these core values. An idealized version of the death penalty might be thought to express respect for human life in the following ways:

1. Through its alleged deterrent and incapacitative effects, it is seen as protecting human life.
2. By virtue of its severity, it is seen as expressing our view that the crime of murder is extraordinarily serious.
3. It is seen as a just punishment if those who impose it are able to judge whether an individual deserves to die for a particular murder and if they impose the death penalty in accord with these justified judgments.[34]

While this ideal version is not immune from criticism, I will not challenge it here. I will accept the view that such an idealized form of the death penalty is logically consistent with a commitment to the value of human life and a certain ideal of justice. A person who cares deeply about these values could affirm the acceptability of an idealized death penalty without contradiction.

The Death Penalty in Practice

The problem is that such an affirmation has little to do with reality. It suffers from a defect that people so fondly cite with respect to utopian positions: "That may work in theory, but it doesn't work in practice." The death penalty that we are concerned about is not just a theory or ideal; it is a practice in the real world. As citizens, we need to know whether it is morally right for our society and its institutions to impose the death penalty. The answer to this question partly depends on abstract beliefs about morality and justice. But just as importantly, it depends on facts about our society and its institutions. Charles Black Jr. makes this point very effectively. He writes:

> We are not presently confronted, as a political society, with the question whether something called "the state" has some abstract right to kill "those who deserve to die." We are confronted by the single unitary question posed by reality: "Shall we kill those who are chosen to be killed by our legal process as it stands?"[35]

On the question of whether the death penalty may be right in some abstract sense, Black adds that "it doesn't really make any difference at all what I think about the abstract rightness of capital punishment. There exists no abstract capital punishment."[36]

While Black's last statement goes too far in denying that there is an "abstract capital punishment," his central point is still very much on target. Black's central point is that the death penalty debate is about a practice and not an abstraction. "Abstract" capital punishment does not kill people. It is the practice of capital punishment—administered by real legal systems and real human beings—that kills people, and we—as citizens of actual societies—have to decide if this practice should continue. Black is entirely correct that these nonabstract questions are the ones we face.

When I speak about an inconsistency in the positions that advocate the death penalty, then I mean an inconsistency between the values affirmed by death penalty supporters and the actual practice of capital punishment. I claim that if death penalty supporters consider their own values, they will see that these values are violated by the institution of capital punishment, both as it exists now and as it is almost certain to exist for the foreseeable future.

Why the Death Penalty Is Inconsistent with the Value of Justice

The death penalty is inconsistent with a concern for justice because we know that the meting out of death as a punishment is not a function of the terribleness of people's crimes and their own degree of culpability. Actual death sentences are the result of arbitrary, irrelevant factors, such as race, social and economic status, and the quality of legal representation. Here are a few facts relevant to these factors.

- In the twenty years following the Supreme Court's 1976 approval of new death penalty laws in *Gregg v. Georgia,* 83 percent of the people executed in the United States were charged with the murder of white victims.[37]
- In the twenty years after *Gregg v. Georgia,* only 1 percent of executions involved white people who had killed black victims.[38]
- According to the U.S. General Accounting Office, a large body of research on race and the death penalty "shows a pattern of evidence indicating racial disparities in the charging, sentencing, and imposition of the death penalty." More than 75 percent of the studies that identified race as a factor in sentencing found that black defendants were more likely to receive the death penalty than members of other racial groups.[39]
- Research on the death penalty in Georgia showed that defendants with court-appointed attorneys were 2.6 times more likely to receive a death sentence than defendants who could afford to hire their own lawyers.[40]
- The same study in Georgia showed that defendants classified as having low socioeconomic status were 2.3 times more likely to receive a death sentence than defendants who were seen as having higher status.
- A *Chicago Tribune* investigation of 285 capital cases in Illinois that the state's death penalty system was pervaded by "bias, error, and incompetence." The *Tribune* cited:
  - large numbers of trial errors, leading appeals courts to reverse roughly half of the death sentences.
  - widespread misconduct by police and prosecutors, including the use of questionable jailhouse-informant testimony in at least forty-six cases.

- ineffective legal representation, as shown by thirty-three cases in which people sentenced to die were represented by lawyers who were later disbarred or suspended.[41]

These problems about legal representation are not limited to Illinois. A report by the American Bar Association (ABA) on the death penalty in the United States cited widespread, serious inadequacies in the provision of lawyers to represent people charged with first-degree murder. These included:

- the appointment of lawyers with no criminal trial experience.
- the appointment of lawyers who do not know the special rules and procedures for trying capital cases.
- the failure of defense lawyers to introduce mitigating factors during the part of the trial devoted to determining the sentence.
- insufficient funds for lawyers to cover the cost of preparing and investigating cases.
- the frequent failure of lawyers to make relevant objections during a trial so that they can be considered on appeal.[42]

The ABA report reached the following conclusion:

In case after case, decisions about who will die and who will live turn not on the nature of the offense the defendant is charged with committing but rather on the nature of the legal representation the defendant receives.[43]

To this factual conclusion, I would add the following moral conclusion. If "decisions about who will die" do not depend on "the nature of the offense the defendant is charged with committing" but are determined by other factors, such as race, social standing, and inadequate legal counsel, then the death penalty as it exists in our society is inconsistent with a commitment to justice.

Death penalty supporters claim they want justice. They say they want people to get the punishment they deserve. Sometimes, in explaining why only some people guilty of homicide should be executed, they add that capital punishment should be restricted to the worst murderers, those whose crimes are most terrible and whose culpability is greatest. What facts like those above show, however, is that the factors that determine whether people are executed differ from the factors cited in defense of the death penalty. Even if justice would be achieved by executing the worst murderers, there is no reason to believe that this is what our system does.

This claim does not depend on official misconduct, abuse, or intentional violation of principles of justice. Suppose, for the sake of argument, that officials in the criminal justice system strive to achieve justice, that police officers, prosecutors, juries, and judges all try to judge defendants fairly and without prejudice. Nonetheless, in spite of their efforts to do justice, their treatment of people is influenced by the race of defendants and victims, by the social standing of defendants and victims, by the ineffective work of court-appointed attorneys. They aim to judge people by what they deserve, but their judgments are nonetheless influenced by factors that have nothing to do with what people deserve. The result is a system in which the punishments imposed on people are significantly influenced by matters that have nothing to do with justice.

From the perspective of justice, such a system is a double failure. It is a failure, first, because it does not achieve the goal of justice—punishing people according to what they deserve. Second, it is a failure because it causes some people to suffer more severe punishments because of their race, social standing, or representation by a substandard lawyer. When this occurs, there is both a failure to achieve the form of justice that is being sought and the active commission of an additional, serious injustice, the imposition of suffering on people for illegitimate reasons.

Of course, these injustices need not lead to a complete rejection of capital punishment if the system could be reformed so as to eliminate the influence of these irrelevant factors. But there is no reason to believe that this can be done. The factors that interfere with achieving justice are too pervasive to be rooted out. They exist at all levels, as shown, for example, by the widespread practice of racial profiling by police and the willingness of courts in many states to assign incompetent lawyers to defendants whose lives are at stake.

Moreover, reforms have already been tried and have failed. In the United States, for more than a quarter of a century attempts have been made to free capital sentencing from the influence of arbitrary factors. This effort is widely regarded as a failure. Supreme Court Justice Harry Blackmun, who had supported the constitutionality of the death penalty in *Furman* and *Gregg*, the landmark cases of the 1970s, came to see its defects as unfixable. In the 1994 case *Callins v. Collins,* Blackmun announced:

From this day forward, I no longer shall tinker with the machinery of death. For more than 20 years I have endeavored . . . along with a majority of this Court to develop procedural and substantive rules that would lend more than the mere appearance of fairness to the death penalty endeavor. . . . I [now] feel morally and intellectually obligated to concede that the death penalty experiment has failed.[44]

Blackmun's experience with reform and the subsequent change in his views are further evidence of the incompatibility between the practice of capital punishment and the value of justice. Anyone who is committed to the value of justice should see that the practice of capital punishment is not compatible with the value they seek. They want justice, but the system actually produces injustice and is likely to continue to do so.

Why the Death Penalty Is Inconsistent with Respect for the Value of Human Life

Having shown why support for the death penalty is inconsistent with a commitment to the value of justice, I will now show why it is inconsistent with respect for the value of human life and, thus, why it should be rejected by anyone who is committed to honoring that value.

In making this argument, I will not appeal to the view that all acts of killing are inconsistent with valuing human life. Like most people, I believe that there are restricted circumstances in which killing and other acts of violence are morally permissible. The death penalty, however, is not one of these circumstances. Instead, the death penalty leads to the acceptance of practices that show a callous disregard for human life that is akin to the disregard shown in acts of murder.

In making this serious charge, I have a number of features of the death penalty system in mind. To begin with, there are the facts that I have cited about the injustice of the death penalty system. Since the quality of legal representation strongly influences the sentence imposed on a person, a system that tolerates inadequate representation for people who may be sentenced to death expresses indifference toward the value of these defendants' lives. There is no way that assigning incompetent lawyers to people in this position can be seen as compatible with a commitment to take seriously the value of each person's life. Nor is the routine failure to provide court-appointed lawyers with the resources to investigate their clients' cases compatible with a commitment to take seriously the value of each person's life. Anyone concerned with the value of human life would be determined to insure that executions occur only after the most exacting procedures have proved beyond a reasonable doubt that death is the proper punishment. There is an obvious inconsistency between affirming the value of human life and tolerating the current level of legal representation for people who face the possibility of death.

Problems of this sort can lead to two kinds of mistakes. The first is that a person who is guilty of a crime may be sentenced to a more severe punishment than would have been received had he or she been a member of a different race, had a higher social status, or had been able to hire a better lawyer. The second is that the poor quality of legal representation may lead to innocent people being convicted and sentenced to die.

While there has been a widespread impression that the U.S. legal system bends over backward to give defendants every conceivable advantage, the facts are quite the opposite. In fact, for many defendants, the system is stacked against them, and the results of the process are not reliable indicators of guilt or innocence. Consider the following facts that set the stage for the moratorium on executions in Illinois.

- Between 1977 and 2000, the state of Illinois both executed twelve people for murder and released from death row thirteen people who had been sentenced to die but were later shown to be innocent.
- In some cases of wrongful convictions, police used coercive measures, including torture, to extract confessions from innocent people.
- In at least forty-six cases, convictions for murder were based on testimony from jailhouse informants; these informants often benefited from their testimony and in some cases had long records of lies and deceit.

The wrongful convictions and sentences were not the product of a fair, but imperfect, system. As the *Chicago Tribune* showed, the circumstances leading to these wrongful convictions included frequent misconduct by police and prosecutors, who presented unreliable evidence to substantiate charges of guilt, as well as flawed court procedures and poor legal representation for defendants.

These kinds of occurrences are not limited to Illinois. According to James McCloskey, from 1973 to 1995, while 226 people were executed in the United States, fifty-four were released from death row after being found innocent of the crimes for which they had been convicted. McCloskey comments:

> This means that during the last twenty years, for every five death row inmates executed, one has been released and exonerated. That points to a rather cracked system, one prone to serious and frequent mistakes.[45]

At the national level, the causes of error also resemble those in Illinois. Hugo Bedau and Michael Radelet identified 350 instances of wrongful convictions in capital cases and found that eighty-four of them resulted from questionable actions by police officers and prosecutors.[46] This is consistent with a general pattern in the causes of wrongful convictions. One study of wrongful convictions in general (that is, not only in homicide cases) concluded:

> If we had to isolate a single "system dynamic" that pervades large numbers of these cases [of erroneous convictions], we would probably describe it as police and prosecutorial overzealousness.[47]

These studies indicate that the flaws in Illinois's system are not unique. The chance of convicting and executing innocent people is substantial, and misconduct by officials in the criminal justice system is a frequent source of error.[48]

While these practices and the resulting convictions of innocent people are dreadful in connection with any cases, they are especially horrifying in the case of the death penalty, since they can result in the execution of people for crimes of which they are innocent. Moreover, the death penalty, when brought to completion, is not a sentence that can be corrected if made in error.

In reply, death penalty supporters may argue that the fact that innocent people were exonerated and released shows that the system works. While errors occur, the possibility of legal appeals

provides a backup system that comes as close as possible to guar-
anteeing that innocent people will not be executed for crimes
they did not commit.

This reply, however, is inconsistent with the facts. First, in
many cases, people have been spared from death only by chance
or through the intervention of people outside the system. In Illinois, one person on death row was released through the work of
students at Chicago-Kent College of Law, while three others were
exonerated after investigations by journalism students at North-
western University. One of these people, Anthony Porter, came
within two days of being executed.[49] Such down-to-the-wire
cases that depend on the fortuitous intervention of outsiders are
not evidence of the reliability or self-correcting nature of the legal
system.

Second, legal appeals generally deal with procedural matters
rather than a review of factual evidence. So, when a case has been
heard at trial and reviewed in numerous appeals, it may nonetheless be the case that the evidence has not been reviewed or reas-
sessed. Unless obviously erroneous factual judgments have been
made, appeals courts generally defer to the original trial judge
and jury for the facts of a case. Errors made at that level are often
difficult to correct, especially if lawyers have not properly
objected to material in the course of the trial.[50]

Moreover, like the rest of us, many people in the legal system
do not like to be shown wrong. Prosecutors who have charged
and convicted people of murder are not happy if it is shown that
they made a mistake. So, when claims of innocence arise, officials
are often resistant to them. As McCloskey notes:

> Once wrongly convicted and sentenced to death, the criminal
> justice system treats you as a leper. No one wants to touch you.
> In my view, those in authority seem to be more interested in
> finality, expediency, speed, and administrative streamlining
> than in truth, justice, and fairness.[51]

McCloskey's claim about the true interests of those in the system
is supported by the ABA report. It portrays a system that seeks to
hasten the execution process rather than to insure that mistakes
have not been made. The ABA report notes that while the federal
government "once funded Post-Conviction Defender Organiza-
tions, which recruited lawyers for death row inmates at the post-

conviction stage, . . . many of those centers have been forced to close because Congress has eliminated their federal funding." The report also points out that the Supreme Court has ruled that "there is no constitutional right to counsel [that is, representation by a lawyer] in post-conviction proceedings, even in capital cases."[52] As a result, people who have new evidence or justified procedural claims may lack the professional assistance that is required to assert claims in a legally credible way.

The lack of interest in correcting mistakes is nowhere more evident than in the time limits set by states for the submission of new evidence and in the Supreme Court's upholding of such limits. In the 1993 case *Herrera v. Collins,* the Court ruled that new evidence in support of a claim of innocence could be disregarded because it had been submitted too late to meet Texas's sixty-day deadline. In defending the constitutionality of executing a person in spite of new evidence of innocence, the Court majority approvingly cited the time limits for submitting new evidence that many states enforce. It noted:

> Texas is one of 17 States that requires a new trial motion based on newly discovered evidence to be made within 60 days of judgment. . . . Eighteen jurisdictions have time limits ranging between 1 and 3 years, with 10 States and the District of Columbia following the 2-year federal time limit. Only 15 States allow a new trial based on newly discovered evidence to be filed more than 3 years after conviction. . . . [Only] 9 States have no time limits.[53]

According to the Court, if new evidence is discovered that shows a person to be innocent, the evidence may be inadmissible because it comes after the deadline for submission—even though the person is facing death.

It is hard to see how the Court's judgment in this case or the state policies that are cited could be consistent with a commitment to respecting human life. What sort of commitment to the value of human life is shown by the sixty-day deadline that Texas and sixteen other states set for submitting new evidence of innocence? Or by the fact that only fifteen states accept evidence after three years? Or that only nine states place no limit on the time period for making sure that people are guilty before being executed? What sort of attitude toward human life is exhibited by a

Supreme Court that places respect for deadlines ahead of a concern about the death of innocent human beings?

No one who is committed to the ideal of respect for human life
could approve of such practices. And yet, these practices are
completely understandable. They reflect the desire of a legal
bureaucracy to get on with its business, to reach finality, to bring
time-consuming appeals to a halt. They reflect the desire of officials not to be shown to have been incompetent, misled, or over-
zealous. They reflect the desire of citizens to have lower taxes
rather than to fund competent lawyers for people charged with
murder. They reflect the fact that it is easier to respect the value
of human life in words than to do so in deeds.

I see no way in which people who are genuinely committed to
respecting the value of human life can consistently support the
death penalty system that we have. At a minimum, they should
be actively involved in efforts to fix this system by supporting
such reforms as making more funds available for expert legal representation for defendants, extensive rights of appeal for defendants, the abolition of time limits for new evidence, and closer
supervision of police and prosecutors. Unfortunately, many
death penalty supporters are on the opposite side of all these
issues. But even if these reforms could be achieved, the influence
of race and social status are likely to play a continuing role in
determining who will be sentenced to die and who will receive
alternative punishments.

Death penalty supporters ought to acknowledge that, even if in
their ideal world the values of justice and human life would be
affirmed by executing murderers, in our actual world, the actual
practice of capital punishment violates these very same values. If
consistency with the values of justice and respect for human life
is the appropriate criterion for deciding the issue, then people
who understand the death penalty system should oppose the
practice of punishing by death. Opposition to the death penalty is
consistent with these values, while support for the death penalty
violates them.

Notes

Chapter 1

1. *The Cunning of History* (New York: Harper & Row, 1978), 87.
2. This argument against pacifism is developed by Jan Narveson in "Pacifism—A Philosophical Analysis," *Ethics* 75 (1965); reprinted in *War and Morality*, edited by R. Wasserstrom (Belmont, Calif.: Wadsworth, 1970).
3. The same argument is made by Cheyney C. Ryan in "Self-Defense, Pacifism, and the Possibility of Killing," *Ethics* 93 (1983): 508–24. Ryan notes, "To get back the washcloth which you have stolen from me, I cannot bludgeon you to death; even if this were the *only* way I had of securing my right to the washcloth, I could not do it."
4. Gen. 4, 14–15.
5. This claim is made by William Bowers and Glen Pierce in "Deterrence or Brutalization: What Is the Effect of Executions?" *Crime and Delinquency* 26 (1980): 453–84; reprinted as chapter 8 of William Bowers, *Legal Homicide* (Boston: Northeastern University Press, 1984).

Chapter 2

1. For a readable review of these sorts of methodological problems, see F. Zimring and G. Hawkins, *Deterrence* (Chicago: University of Chicago Press, 1973), 23–33, 249–57.
2. From *The Death Penalty* (Philadelphia: American Law Institute, 1959); reprinted in *The Death Penalty in America*, rev. ed., edited by H. Bedau (Garden City, N.Y.: Anchor Books, 1967), 276.
3. Sellin, in Bedau, 1967 ed., 279.
4. The table is from David Baldus and James Cole, "A Comparison of the Work of Thorstein Sellin and Isaac Ehrlich on the Deterrent Effect of Capital Punishment," *Yale Law Journal* 85 (1975): 171.
5. For charts showing these annual trends, see Sellin, in Bedau, 1967 ed., 280–83.
6. This study is also reprinted in Bedau, 284–301.
7. Ehrlich presented his view in "The Deterrent Effect of Capital Punishment: A Question of Life and Death," *American Economic Review* 65 (1975): 397–417.
8. Quoted in H. Bedau, ed., *The Death Penalty in America*, 3d ed. (New York: Oxford University Press, 1982), 96.
9. In Baldus and Cole, 180.
10. See Peter Passell and John Taylor, "The Deterrent Effect of Capital Punishment: Another View," *American Economic Review* 67 (1977): 448.

11. Peter Passell, "The Deterrent Effect of Capital Punishment: A Statistical Test," *Stanford Law Review* 28 (1975): 61–80.

12. For a graph showing the execution and homicide rates in the 1960s, see Hans Zeisel, "The Deterrent Effect of the Death Penalty: Facts v. Faith," in *The Supreme Court Review 1976*, edited by Philip Kurland (Chicago: University of Chicago Press, 1977), 317–43, reprinted in Bedau, 3d ed., 127.

13. *Neither Cruel Nor Unusual* (New Rochelle, N.Y.: Arlington, 1978), 54.

14. On the effect of the moratorium, see W. Bowers, *Legal Homicide* (Boston: Northeastern University Press, 1984) 106–14; and Zeisel, in Bedau, 3d edition, 131–33.

15. Bowers, 289, 298.

16. Ibid., 330–33.

17. Bedau, "Recidivism, Parole, and Deterrence," in Bedau, ed., 3d ed., 175.

18. "The Deterrent Effect of the Death Penalty upon Prison Murder," in Bedau, 3d ed., 159–73.

Chapter 3

1. Barry Nakell, "The Cost of the Death Penalty," *Criminal Law Bulletin* 14 (1978): 68–80; reprinted in H. Bedau, ed., *The Death Penalty in America*, 3d ed. (New York: Oxford University Press, 1982), 241–46.

2. "The Cost of Taking a Life: Dollars and Sense of the Death Penalty," *U.C. Davis Law Review* 18 (1985): 1257–58.

3. Ibid., 1258.

4. *Capital Losses: The Price of the Death Penalty in New York State* (Albany, N.Y.: New York State Defenders Association, 1982), 19.

5. Garey, "The Cost of Taking a Life: Dollars and Sense of the Death Penalty," *U.C. Davis Law Review* 18 (1985), 1261.

6. See Bedau, 3d ed., 193.

7. Ibid., 246.

8. For a discussion that emphasizes the connection between judicial processes and respect for human life, see Margaret J. Radin, "Cruel Punishment and Respect for Persons: Super Due Process for Death," *Southern California Law Review* 53 (1980): 1143–85; reprinted in *Punishment and Rehabilitation*, 2d ed., edited by J. Murphy (Belmont, Calif.: Wadsworth, 1985), 134–68.

9. Cambridge, Mass.: Harvard University Press, 1971, 12.

Chapter 4

1. *Capital Punishment: The Inevitability of Caprice and Mistake*, 2d ed. (New York: Norton, 1981), 20.

2. From *Furman v. Georgia*, 408 U.S. 239 (1972); reprinted in H. Bedau, *The Death Penalty in America*, 3d ed. (New York: Oxford University Press, 1982), 263–64; emphasis added.

3. For extensive evidence of racial discrimination in the imposition of the death penalty, see W. Bowers, *Legal Homicide* (Boston: Northeastern University Press, 1984), chs. 3 and 7.

4. Reprinted in Bedau, 3d ed., 255.

5. 428 U.S. 280–324 (1976); excerpted in Bedau, 3d ed., 288–293.
6. "The Collapse of the Case Against Capital Punishment," *National Review*, March 31, 1978, 397. A briefer version of this paper appeared in the *Criminal Law Bulletin* 14 (1978): 51–68 and is reprinted in Bedau, 3d ed., 323–33.
7. Ibid., emphasis added.
8. Black, 29.
9. For an interesting account of a case in which classification problems emerge quite vividly, see Steven Phillips, *No Heroes, No Villains* (New York: Random House, 1977).
10. For historical material about the United States, see William Bowers, *Legal Homicide*, part I.
11. For this evidence, see Charles Black, *Capital Punishment*, passim; William Bowers and Glen Pierce, "Racial Discrimination and Criminal Homicide under Post-*Furman* Statutes," in W. Bowers, *Legal Homicide*, ch. 7, and reprinted in Bedau, 3d ed., 206–23; Ursula Bentele, "The Death Penalty in Georgia: Still Arbitrary," *Washington University Law Quarterly* 62 (1985): 573–646; and Samuel Gross and Robert Mauro, "Patterns of Death: An Analysis of Racial Disparities in Capital Sentencing and Homicide Victimization," *Stanford Law Review* 37 (1984): 27–153.
12. For a chart showing these figures in full, see Bowers, 225; reprinted in Bedau, 3d ed., 213.
13. On this point, see Bentele, 615.

Chapter 5

1. In H. Bedau, *The Death Penalty in America*, 3d ed. (New York: Oxford University Press, 1982), 255–56.
2. Some of the difficulties here are illuminated by Joel Feinberg's distinction between "comparative" and "noncomparative" criteria of justice. For his discussion, see "Noncomparative Justice," in *Rights, Justice, and the Bounds of Liberty: Essays in Social Philosophy* (Princeton, N.J.: Princeton University Press, 1980); originally published in the *Philosophical Review* 83 (1974): 297–338.
3. "The Collapse of the Case Against Capital Punishment," *National Review*, March 31, 1978, 397.
4. For discussions of arbitrariness and discrimination as general problems, see The American Friends Service Committee, *Struggle for Justice* (New York: Hill & Wang, 1971); and Willard Gaylin, *Partial Justice: A Study of Bias in Sentencing* (New York: Vintage Books, 1975).

Chapter 6

1. As Joel Feinberg has written, "desert is a *moral* concept in the sense that it is logically prior to and independent of public institutions and their rules." See "Justice and Personal Desert," in *Doing and Deserving* (Princeton, N.J.: Princeton University Press, 1970), 87.
2. Kant, *Metaphysical Elements of Justice*, translated by John Ladd (Indianapolis: Bobbs-Merrill, 1965), 101.
3. *Doing Justice* (New York: Hill & Wang, 1976), 66; reprinted in *Sentencing*, edited by H. Gross and A. von Hirsch (Oxford University Press,

1981), 243. For a more recent discussion and further defense by von Hirsch, see his *Past or Future Crimes* (New Brunswick, N.J.: Rutgers University Press, 1985).

4. von Hirsch, *Doing Justice,* 93–94. My criticisms of proportional retributivism are not novel. For helpful discussions of the view, see Hugo Bedau, "Concessions to Retribution in Punishment," in *Justice and Punishment,* edited by J. Cederblom and W. Blizek (Cambridge, Mass.: Ballinger, 1977), and M. Golding, *Philosophy of Law* (Englewood Cliffs, N.J.: Prentice Hall, 1975), 98–99.

5. See von Hirsch, *Past and Future Crimes,* ch. 8.

6. For more positive assessments of these theories, see Jeffrey Reiman, "Justice, Civilization, and the Death Penalty," *Philosophy and Public Affairs* 14 (1985): 115–48; and Michael Davis, "How to Make the Punishment Fit the Crime," *Ethics* 93 (1983).

7. Consider the following more representative statement by Kant: "To be beneficent when we can is a duty; and besides this, there are many minds so sympathetically constituted that . . . they find a pleasure in spreading joy around them, and can take delight in the satisfaction of others so far as it is their own work. But I maintain that in such a case an action of this kind, however proper, however amiable it may be, has nevertheless no true moral worth. . . . For the maxim lacks the moral import, namely, that such actions be done *from duty*, not from inclination." See *Fundamental Principles of the Metaphysic of Morals,* translated by T. Abbott (New York: Liberal Arts Press, 1949), 15–16.

8. The Court struck down mandatory death sentences in *Woodson v. North Carolina,* 428 U.S. 280–324 (1976).

Chapter 7

1. In presenting this account, I am indebted to Elizabeth Lane Beardsley's illuminating paper "Moral Worth and Moral Credit," *Philosophical Review* 66 (1957), especially 306–7; reprinted in *Moral Philosophy,* edited by J. Feinberg and H. West (Belmont, Calif.: Dickenson, 1977).

2. "Moral Worth and Moral Credit," 313.

3. Beardsley herself does not reach this conclusion. She believes that there are different types of desert judgments which are independent of one another and rejects the view that one type is basic. On this, see both the paper "Moral Worth and Moral Credit," which I have already cited, as well as her "Determinism and Moral Perspectives," *Philosophy and Phenomenological Research* 21 (1960).

4. A. von Hirsch, *Doing Justice* (New York: Hill & Wang, 1976), 177.

5. On these issues, see John Hospers, "What Means This Freedom?" in *Determinism and Freedom in the Age of Science,* edited by S. Hook (New York: Collier Books, 1971).

6. *The Constitution of Liberty* (Chicago: Regnery, 1972), 95.

7. The idea of a precise scale is criticized by Joel Feinberg in his essays "Supererogation and Rules" and "Problematic Responsibility in Law and Morals," in *Doing and Deserving* (Princeton, N.J.: Princeton University Press, 1970).

8. My argument here is indebted to Richard Brandt, "Determinism and the Justifiability of Moral Blame," in S. Hook, ed., *Determinism and Freedom in the Age of Modern Science.*

Chapter 8

1. On the contemporary use of torture, see the various publications of Amnesty International.

2. See, for example, *Weems v. United States* 217 U.S. 357 (1909) and *Trop v. Dulles* 356 U.S. 86 (1958).

3. In H. Bedau, *The Death Penalty in America*, 3d ed. (Oxford University Press, 1982), 257.

4. Ibid., 265.

5. It is worth noting that Justice White voted to reinstate the death penalty in *Gregg v. Georgia*. He was persuaded that the new laws would prevent arbitrariness and therefore that they were in accord with the Constitution. Since he does not discuss the issue of excessive levels of punishment, he may have rejected or forgotten his own previous argument.

6. For some comparisons, see Ursula Bentele, "The Death Penalty in Georgia: Still Arbitrary," *Washington University Law Quarterly* 62 (1985): 585–91.

7. The connections between the death penalty and the "moralistic" conception of the state emerge very clearly in Walter Berns, *For Capital Punishment* (New York: Basic Books, 1979). The classic liberal case for the restricted state is expressed in John Stuart Mill, *On Liberty*. Mill himself, however, favored the death penalty.

8. For similar ideas, see American Friends Service Committee, *Struggle for Justice* (New York: Hill & Wang, 1971), 117–20, 145–51; and Ronald Dworkin, "Liberalism," in *Public & Private Morality*, edited by S. Hampshire (New York: Oxford University Press, 1978).

9. For a careful analysis of "cruel and unusual" and a combined moral and constitutional attack on the death penalty, see Hugo Bedau, "Thinking of the Death Penalty as a Cruel and Unusual Punishment," *U.C. Davis Law Review* 18 (1985): 873–925.

Chapter 9

1. Quoted in Ernest van den Haag, *Punishing Criminals* (New York: Basic Books, 1975), 11.

2. *Punishing Criminals*, 13.

3. For the data on lynchings and executions, see W. Bowers, *Legal Homicide* (Boston: Northeastern University Press, 1985), 54.

4. Locke, ch. 9, section 125.

5. I owe this positive feature of vengeance to Susan Jacoby's defense of vengeance in *Wild Justice: The Evolution of Revenge* (New York: Harper & Row, 1983). See, too, Andrew Oldenquist, "The Case for Revenge," *The Public Interest* 82 (Winter 1986): 72–80.

Chapter 10

1. For an attempt to show that executions are inhumane in the same way that torture is, see Jeffrey Reiman, "Justice, Civilization, and the Death Penalty," *Philosophy and Public Affairs* 14 (1985): 134–42.

2. One noteworthy example is Peter Singer, *Practical Ethics* (Cambridge: Cambridge University Press, 1979), ch. 8.

3. H. Bedau and M. Radelet, "Miscarriages of Justice in Potentially Capital Cases," forthcoming in *Stanford Law Review* 39 (1987).

4. "The Death Penalty in Georgia: Still Arbitrary." *Washington University Law Quarterly* 62 (1985): 597–600.

5. For a powerful and illuminating discussion of these issues, the reader is again referred to Charles Black, *Capital Punishment: The Inevitability of Caprice and Mistake,* 2d ed. (New York: Norton, 1981).

6. For some comparisons of cases, see U. Bentele, "The Death Penalty in Georgia: Still Arbitrary," *Washington University Law Quarterly* 62 (1985): 585–91.

7. H. Bedau, *The Death Penalty in America,* 3d ed. (New York: Oxford University Press, 1982), Table 2-3-2.

8. Charles Black argues against the relevance of several imaginary and hypothetical situations in *Capital Punishment: The Inevitability of Caprice and Mistake,* 2d ed. (New York: Norton, 1981), 157–74.

Chapter 11

1. From "In Defense of the Death Penalty: A Legal—Practical—Moral Analysis," in H. Bedau, *The Death Penalty in America,* 3d ed. (New York: Oxford University Press, 1982), 332.

2. Walter Berns, *For Capital Punishment* (New York: Basic Books, 1979), 155; reprinted in Bedau, 3rd ed., 335–36.

3. Ibid., 172–73.

4. *Fundamental Principles of the Metaphysics of Morals,* translated by T. Abbott (New York: Liberal Arts Press, 1949), 46.

Postscripts to the Second Edition Notes

1. For reflections on public opinion about the death penalty and issues of crime generally, see Wendy Kaminer, *It's All the Rage* (Reading, Mass.: Addison Wesley, 1995).

2. Gallup Poll Organization, *www.gallup.com/poll/indicators/ind death_pen.asp* (June 12, 2001).

3. On Governor Ryan's decision, see K. Armstrong and S. Mills, "Ryan: Until I Can Be Sure—Illinois Is First State to Suspend Death Penalty," *Chicago Tribune,* February 1, 2000, as well as Ryan's press release, which is available at www.state.il.us/gov/press/00/Jan/morat.htm (June 12, 2001).

4. For a description of this trend, see F. Zimring and G. Hawkins, *Capital Punishment and the American Agenda* (Cambridge: Cambridge University Press, 1986), ch. 1. The South African court ruling came in *State v. Makwanyane,* 1995.

5. Zimring and Hawkins, writing in 1986, did predict the end of capital punishment in the United States, claiming it was more likely to occur "in fifteen years than in fifty years . . . [and possibly] in the near future." See *Capital Punishment and the American Agenda,* 157.

6. *State v. Makwanyane,* 1995, section 348.

7. Popper, *The Open Society and Its Enemies,* vol. 2, 5th rev. ed. (Princeton, N.J.: Princeton University Press, 1966), 234.

8. On the historical background, see H. A. Bedau, *The Death Penalty in America,* rev. ed. (New York: Anchor Doubleday, 1967), 1–7. The reference to America's first execution is from Lloyd Steffens, *Executing Justice* (Cleveland, Ohio: Pilgrim Press, 1998), 32.

9. William Bowers, *Legal Homicide: Death As Punishment in America, 1864–1982* (Boston: Northeastern University Press, 1984), 9.

10. Amitai Etzioni, *The New Golden Rule* (New York: Basic Books, 1996), 106–7.

11. For a now classic description of nonrational factors in science, see T. S. Kuhn, *The Structure of Scientific Revolutions* (Chicago: University of Chicago Press, 1962). Regarding the influence of reason on the passions, David Hume, though he described reason as the "slave of the passions," acknowledged that if desires are based on false beliefs, then "The moment we perceive the falsehood of any supposition, . . . our passions yield to our reason without any opposition." See his *A Treatise of Human Nature,* book 2, part 2, section 3 (Oxford: Oxford University Press, 1888). For a general discussion of rationality, see Stephen Nathanson, *The Ideal of Rationality: A Defense Within Reason* (Chicago: Open Court, 1994).

12. P. Ellsworth and S. Gross, "Second Thoughts: Americans' Views on the Death Penalty at the Turn of the Century," in *Capital Punishment at Century's End: New Insights, Old Doubts,* ed. Stephen P. Garvey (Durham, N.C.: Duke University Press, forthcoming, 2001).

13. Gallup Poll Organization, www.gallup.com/poll/indicators/ind death_pen.asp (June 12, 2001).

14. When people appear to shift their views, one of two things may be happening. Question number 2 may be reminding them of an alternative that they already favored but had overlooked in their response to question number 1; or question number 2 may cause them to change their minds by offering an alternative of which they had not previously been aware.

15. For criticism of the standard polling question and more sophisticated measures of public opinion, see W. Bowers, M. Vandiver, and P. Dugan, "A New Look at Public Opinion on Capital Punishment: What Citizens and Legislators Prefer," *American Journal of Criminal Law* 22 (1994): 77–149.

16. William Bowers, "Capital Punishment and Contemporary Values: People's Misgivings and the Court's Misperceptions," *Law & Society Review* 27 (1993): 165–86.

17. Bowers, "Capital Punishment and Contemporary Values," 168.

18. Bowers, "Capital Punishment and Contemporary Values," 167.

19. Bowers, "Capital Punishment and Contemporary Values," 163.

20. P. Ellsworth and S. Gross, "Hardening of the Attitudes: Americans' Views on the Death Penalty," in *The Death Penalty in America: Current Controversies,* ed. H. A. Bedau (New York: Oxford University Press, 1997), 98.

21. Ellsworth and Gross, "Hardening of the Attitudes," 107. On the high level of ignorance about the death penalty, see as well Kaminer, *It's All the Rage.*

22. For an insightful description of belief change and the inherent conservatism of believers, see William James, *Pragmatism* (Indianapolis: Hackett, 1981), 31 (in Lecture II, "What Pragmatism Means"). This phenomenon is discussed by Gilbert Harman in *Change in View* (Cambridge, Mass.: MIT Press, 1986).

23. See Ellsworth and Gross, "Second Thoughts."

24. For comparisons between moral judgments about war and the death penalty, see Stephen Nathanson, "The Death Penalty As a Peace Issue," in D. Curtin and R. Litke, eds., *Institutional Violence* (Amsterdam: Rodopi, 2000), 53–59; and Steffens, *Executing Justice.*

25. Even if executing murderers restored victims to life, the death penalty would remain troubling. Suppose, for example, that victims were restored to life only when their actual murderers were executed. If the wrong person were executed, the victim would remain dead, and we would know immediately that an erroneous execution had occurred. This would put enormous pressure on officials to make sure that they were executing the right person. So, even in this fantastic case, there would still be a death penalty debate.

26. I argue for the nonabstract character of the death penalty debate in "How (Not) to Think about the Death Penalty," *International Journal of Applied Philosophy* (11 Winter/Spring 1997): 7–10.

27. Descartes, *Rules for the Direction of the Mind*, Rule II, in E. Haldane and G. Ross, trans., *The Philosophical Works of Descartes*, vol. 1 (New York: Dover Publications), 3.

28. The same reasoning was used by logical positivists and other emotivists to show that reason cannot settle any ethical disputes. For classic expressions of this view, see A. J. Ayer, *Language, Truth, and Logic* (New York: Dover Publications, 1946), ch. 6; and C. L. Stevenson, "The Nature of Ethical Disagreement," in *Fact and Values* (New Haven, Conn.: Yale University Press, 1963), 1–9.

29. For a recent review of the literature on deterrence, see W. Bailey and R. Peterson, "Murder, Capital Punishment, and Deterrence: A Review of the Literature," in *The Death Penalty in America: Current Controversies*, ed. H. A. Bedau (New York: Oxford University Press, 1997).

30. David Hume, *A Treatise of Human Nature*, book 1, part 4, section 1, Selby-Bigge edition (Oxford: Oxford University Press, 1888), 186.

31. Jeff Goodell, "Letting Go of McVeigh," *New York Times Magazine*, May 13, 2001, 43.

32. My discussion ignores many aspects of these issues. For other discussions that are relevant to questions about disagreement and belief change, see T. S. Kuhn, *The Structure of Scientific Revolutions* (Chicago: University of Chicago Press, 1962), and Murray Edelman, *Constructing the Political Spectacle* (Chicago: University of Chicago Press, 1988).

33. Ellsworth and Gross claim that one of the virtues of the moratorium proposal is that people can support a moratorium on the death penalty without fully renouncing their view that the death penalty is desirable. See their "Second Thoughts."

34. This is not a complete description of the requirements of justice. See chapters 4 and 5 for discussion of some other factors.

35. Charles Black Jr., *Capital Punishment: The Inevitability of Caprice and Mistake*, 2nd ed. (New York: W. W. Norton, 1981), 166.

36. Black, *Capital Punishment*, 166.

37. Roger Hood, "Capital Punishment," in *The Handbook of Criminal Justice*, ed. M. Tonry, (New York: Oxford University Press, 1998), 745.

38. Ibid.

39. U. S. General Accounting Office, *The Death Penalty in America: Current Controversies*, ed. H. A. Bedau (New York: Oxford University Press, 1997), 272.

40. D. Baldus, G. Woodworth, and C. Pulaski Jr., *Equal Justice and the Death Penalty* (Boston: Northeastern University Press, 1990); 158. See, too, Stephen Bright, "Counsel for the Poor: The Death Sentence Not for the Worst Crime but for the Worst Lawyer," in *The Death Penalty in America: Current Controversies,* ed. H. A. Bedau (New York: Oxford University Press, 1997) 275–309.

41. Armstrong and Mills, "Ryan: Until I Can Be Sure."

42. American Bar Association Report, approved by the ABA House of Delegates, February 3, 1997, 7–9; accessible at www.abanet.org/irr/rpt107.html (June 12, 2001).

43. ABA Report, 6.

44. Blackmun, quoted in H. A. Bedau, ed., *The Death Penalty in America: Current Controversies* (New York: Oxford University Press, 1997), 243.

45. James McCloskey, "The Death Penalty: A Personal View," *Criminal Justice Ethics* 2 (Summer/Fall 1996), 70. McCloskey cites a 1993 House Judiciary Committee report as the source of his data.

46. H. Bedau and M. Radelet, "Miscarriages of Justice in Potentially Capital Cases," *Stanford Law Review* 40 (1987): 21–179; see also their later work, with C. E. Putnam, *In Spite of Innocence* (Boston: Northeastern University Press, 1992).

47. C. Ronald Huff, Arye Rattner, and Edward Sagarin, *Convicted Innocent: Wrongful Convictions and Public Policy* (Thousand Oaks, Calif.: Sage, 1996), 64.

48. Official misconduct is not the only source of errors. For an analysis of a variety of sources of inaccuracy in criminal cases and proposals to increase accuracy, see Daniel Givelber, "Meaningless Acquittals, Meaningful Convictions: Do We Reliably Acquit the Innocent?" *Rutgers Law Review* 49 (1997): 1317–96.

49. Armstrong and Mills, "Ryan: Until I Can Be Sure."

50. On this point, see U. Bentele and E. Cary, *Appellate Advocacy: Principles and Practice* (Cincinnati, Ohio: Anderson, 1990), 72–73.

51. McCloskey, "The Death Penalty: A Personal View," 70.

52. ABA Report, 9.

53. *Herrera v. Collins*, 506 U.S. 390 (1993); text accompanying notes 8–11.

Updated Bibliography

American Bar Association. 1997. Report No. 107. Website: www.abanet.org/irr/rpt107.html (June 12, 2001).

American Friends Service Committee. 1971. *Struggle for Justice.* New York: Hill & Wang.

Amnesty International. 1987. *United States of America: The Death Penalty.* London: Amnesty International Publications.

Armstrong, Ken, and Steve Mills. 1999. "Failure of the Death Penalty in Illinois: A Five-Part Series." *Chicago Tribune,* November 14–18, 1999.

Bailey, W., and R. Peterson. 1997. "Murder, Capital Punishment, and Deterrence: A Review of the Literature." In *The Death Penalty in America: Current Controversies,* edited by Hugo Adam Bedau (135–61). New York: Oxford University Press.

Baldus, D., and J. Cole. 1975. "A Comparison of the Work of Thorstein Sellin and Isaac Ehrlich on the Deterrent Effect of Capital Punishment." *Yale Law Journal* 85: 170–86.

Baldus, D., G. Woodworth, and C. Pulaski Jr. 1990. *Equal Justice and the Death Penalty.* Boston: Northeastern University Press.

Beardsley, Elizabeth. 1957. "Moral Worth and Moral Credit." *Philosophical Review* 66: 304–28.

———. 1960. "Determinism and Moral Perspectives." *Philosophy and Phenomenological Research* 21.

Bedau, Hugo, ed. 1967. *The Death Penalty in America,* rev. ed. Garden City, N.Y.: Anchor Books.

———. 1970. "The Death Penalty as a Deterrent: Argument and Evidence." *Ethics* 80: 205–17.

———. 1978. "Retribution and the Theory of Punishment." *Journal of Philosophy* 75: 601–20.

———. 1980. "Capital Punishment." In *Matters of Life and Death,* edited by T. Regan. New York: Random House.

———, ed. 1982. *The Death Penalty in America,* 3d ed. New York: Oxford University Press.

———. 1985. "Thinking of Death as a Cruel and Unusual Punishment." *U.C. Davis Law Review* 18: 873–926.

———. 1987. *Death Is Different.* Boston: Northeastern University Press.

———, ed. 1997. *The Death Penalty in America: Current Controversies.* New York: Oxford University Press.

———. 1999. "Abolishing the Death Penalty Even for the Worst Murderers." In *The Killing State,* edited by Austin Sarat. New York: Oxford University Press.

———. n.d. *The Case against the Death Penalty.* Washington, D.C.: American Civil Liberties Union.

Selected Bibliography

Bedau, Hugo, and Michael Radelet. 1987. "Miscarriages of Justice in Potentially Capital Cases." *Stanford Law Review* 39.

Bentele, Ursula. 1985. "The Death Penalty in Georgia: Still Arbitrary." *Washington University Law Quarterly* 62: 573–676.

———. 1998. "Back to an International Perspective on the Death Penalty As a Cruel Punishment: The Case of South Africa," *Tulane Law Review* 73: 251–304.

Bentele, Ursula, and Eve Cary. 1990. *Appellate Advocacy: Principles and Practice.* Cincinnati, Ohio: Anderson.

Berns, Walter. 1979. *For Capital Punishment.* New York: Basic Books.

Black, Charles. 1981. *Capital Punishment: The Inevitability of Caprice and Mistake,* 2d ed. New York: Norton.

Bohm, Robert. 1999. *Deathquest.* Cincinnati, Ohio: Anderson.

Bowers, William. 1984. *Legal Homicide.* Boston: Northeastern University Press.

———. 1993. "Capital Punishment and Contemporary Values: People's Misgivings and the Court's Misperceptions," *Law & Society Review* 27: 165–86.

———. 1995. "The Capital Jury Project: Rationale, Design, and Preview of Early Findings," *Indiana Law Journal* 70: 1043–102.

Bowers, William, and Glen Pierce. 1980. "Racial Discrimination and Criminal Homicide Under Post-*Furman* Capital Statutes." *Crime and Delinquency* 26: 563–635.

———. 1980. "Deterrence or Brutalization: What Is the Effect of Executions?" *Crime and Delinquency* 26: 453–84.

Bowers, William, Margaret Vandiver, and Patricia Dugan. 1994. "A New Look at Public Opinion on Capital Punishment: What Citizens and Legislators Prefer," *American Journal of Criminal Law* 22: 77–149.

Brandt, Richard. 1961. "Determinism and the Justifiability of Moral Blame." In *Determinism and Freedom in the Age of Modern Science,* edited by Sidney Hook. New York: Collier Books.

Calabresi, Guido. 1985. *Ideals, Beliefs, Attitudes, and the Law.* Syracuse, N.Y.: Syracuse University Press.

Camus, Albert. 1960. "Reflections on the Guillotine." In *Resistance, Rebellion, and Death,* translated by Justin O'Brien. New York: Modern Library.

Carrington, Frank. 1978. *Neither Cruel Nor Unusual.* New Rochelle, N.Y.: Arlington.

Conrad, John, and Ernest van den Haag. 1983. *The Death Penalty: A Debate.* New York: Plenum.

Conway, David. 1974. "Capital Punishment and Deterrence." *Philosophy and Public Affairs* 3: 431–43.

Currie, Elliot. 1985. *Confronting Crime: An American Challenge.* New York: Pantheon Books.

Davis, Michael. 1996. *Justice in the Shadow of Death.* Lanham, Md.: Rowman & Littlefield.

———. 1997. "The Justification of Arbitrary Death," *International Journal of Applied Philosophy* 11(2): 1–6.

Death Penalty Information Center. Website: www.deathpenaltyinfo.org/ (June 12, 2001).

Dolinko, David. 1986. "Foreword: How to Criticize the Death Penalty," *The Journal of Criminal Law & Criminology* 77: 546–601.

Selected Bibliography

Ehrlich, Isaac. 1975. "The Deterrent Effect of Capital Punishment: A Question of Life and Death." *American Economic Review* 65: 397–417.

Ellsworth, P., and S. Gross. 1994. "Hardening of the Attitudes: Americans' Views on the Death Penalty," *Journal of Social Issues* 50(2): 19–52. Reprinted in *The Death Penalty in America: Current Controversies,* edited by Hugo Adam Bedau. New York: Oxford University Press, 1997.

———. 2001. "Second Thoughts: Americans' Views on the Death Penalty at the Turn of the Century." In *Capital Punishment at Century's End: New Insights, Old Doubts,* edited by S. P. Garvey. Durham, N.C.: Duke University Press.

Feinberg, Joel. 1970. *Doing and Deserving.* Princeton: Princeton University Press.

Garey, Margot. 1985. "The Cost of Taking a Life: Dollars and Sense of the Death Penalty." *U.C. Davis Law Review* 18: 1271–74.

Gaylin, Willard. 1975. *Partial Justice: A Study of Bias in Sentencing.* New York: Vintage Books.

———. 1983. *The Killing of Bonnie Garland.* New York: Penguin.

Gert, Bernard. 1973. *The Moral Rules.* New York: Harper & Row.

Givelber, Daniel. 1997. "Meaningless Acquittals, Meaningful Convictions: Do We Reliably Acquit the Innocent?" *Rutgers Law Review* 49(4): 1317–96.

Glover, Jonathan. 1977. *Causing Deaths and Saving Lives.* New York: Penguin.

Grisham, John. 1994. *The Chamber.* New York: Dell.

Gross, Samuel, and Robert Mauro. 1989. *Death and Discrimination.* Boston: Northeastern University Press.

———. "Patterns of Death: An Analysis of Disparities in Capital Sentencing and Homicide Victimization." *Stanford Law Review* 37: 27–153.

Haines, Herbert. 1996. *Against Capital Punishment: The Anti-Death Penalty Movement in America, 1972–1994.* New York: Oxford University Press.

Hart, H.L.A. 1968. *Punishment and Responsibility.* New York: Oxford University Press.

Hayek, Friedrich. 1960. *The Constitution of Liberty.* Chicago: University of Chicago Press.

Hood, Roger. 1998. "Capital Punishment." In *The Handbook of Criminal Justice,* edited by M. Tonry. New York: Oxford University Press.

Hospers, John. 1961. "What Means This Freedom?" In *Determinism and Freedom in the Age of Science,* edited by Sidney Hook. New York: Collier Books.

Huff, C. Ronald, Arye Rattner, and Edward Sagarin. 1996. *Convicted but Innocent: Wrongful Convictions and Public Policy.* Thousand Oaks, Calif.: Sage.

Jacoby, Susan. 1983. *Wild Justice: The Evolution of Revenge.* New York: Harper & Row.

Kaminer, Wendy. 1995. *It's All the Rage.* Reading, Mass.: Addison Wesley.

Kant, Imanuel. 1949. *Fundamental Principles of the Metaphysic of Morals,* translated by T. Abbott. New York: Liberal Arts Press.

———. 1965. *Metaphysical Principles of Justice,* translated by John Ladd. Indianapolis: Bobbs-Merrill.

Kleinig, John. 1971. "The Concept of Desert." *American Philosophical Quarterly* 8.

———. 1973. *Punishment and Desert.* Dordrecht, Netherlands: Reidel.

Lempert, Richard. 1981. "Desert and Deterrence: An Assessment of the Moral Bases of the Case for Capital Punishment." *Michigan Law Review* 79: 1177–1231.

Liebman, James, Jeffrey Fagan, and Valerie West. "A Broken System: Error Rates in Capital Cases, 1975–1995. Website: justice.policy.net/jpreport/ (June 12, 2001).

Locke, John. 1689. *Two Treatises of Government.*

McCloskey, James. 1996. "The Death Penalty: A Personal View," *Criminal Justice Ethics* 2, Summer/Fall: 69–75.

Meltsner, Michael. 1973. *Cruel and Unusual: The Supreme Court and Capital Punishment.* New York: Random House.

Mill, J.S. 1859. *On Liberty.*

Montague, Phillip. 1995. *Punishment As Societal Defense.* Lanham, Md.: Rowman & Littlefield.

Murphy, Jeffrie. 1973. "Marxism and Retribution." *Philosophy and Public Affairs* 2: 218–43.

Nakell, Barry. 1978. "The Cost of the Death Penalty." *Criminal Law Bulletin* 14: 68–80.

Nakell, Barry, and Kenneth Hardy. 1987. *The Arbitrariness of the Death Penalty.* Philadelphia: Temple University Press.

Narveson, Jan. 1965. "Pacifism—A Philosophical Analysis." *Ethics* 75: 259–71.

Nathanson, Stephen. 1985. "Does It Matter if the Death Penalty Is Arbitrarily Administered?" *Philosophy and Public Affairs* 14: 149–64.

———. 1997. "How (Not) to Think about the Death Penalty," *International Journal of Applied Philosophy,* 11(2): 7–10.

———. 1997. "An Eye for an Eye? The Immorality of Punishing by Death." In *Ethics for Today and Tomorrow,* edited by Joram Haber. Boston: Jones & Bartlett.

———. 2000. "Is the Death Penalty What Murderers Deserve?" In *Living Morally,* edited by S. Luper. New York: Harcourt Brace.

———. 2000. "The Death Penalty As a Peace Issue." In *Institutional Violence,* edited by D. Curtin and R. Litke. Amsterdam: Rodopi.

———. 2000. "Capital Punishment." In *The Philosophy of Law: An Encyclopedia,* edited by C. Gray. New York: Garland.

New York State Defenders Association. 1982. *Capital Losses: The Price of the Death Penalty in New York State.* Albany, N.Y.

Oldenquist, Andrew. 1986. "The Case for Revenge." *The Public Interest* 82 (Winter): 72–80.

Passell, Peter. 1975. "The Deterrent Effect of Capital Punishment: A Statistical Test." *Stanford Law Review* 28: 61–80.

Passell, Peter, and John Taylor. 1977. "The Deterrent Effect of Capital Punishment: Another View." *American Economic Review* 67.

Phillips, Steven. 1977. *No Heroes, No Villains.* New York: Random House.

Pierce, Glenn, and Michael Radelet. 1990. "The Role and Consequences of the Death Penalty in American Politics," *Review of Law & Social Change* 18: 711–28.

Pojman, Louis, and Jeffrey Reiman. 1998. *The Death Penalty: For and Against.* Lanham, Md.: Rowman & Littlefield.

Prejean, Helen. 1993. *Dead Man Walking: An Eyewitness Account of the Death Penalty in America.* New York: Random House.

Radelet, Michael, Hugo Adam Bedau, and Constance E. Putnam. 1992. *In Spite of Innocence*. Boston: Northeastern University Press.
Radin, Margaret. 1978. "The Jurisprudence of Death: Evolving Standards for the Cruel and Unusual Punishments Clause." *University of Pennsylvania Law Review* 126: 989–1064.
———. 1980. "Cruel Punishment and Respect for Persons: Super Due Process for Death." *Southern California Law Review* 53: 1143–85.
———. 1985. "Proportionality, Subjectivity, and Tragedy." *U.C. Davis Law Review* 18: 1165–77.
Rawls, John. 1955. "Two Concepts of Rules." *Philosophical Review* 64: 2–32.
———. 1971. *A Theory of Justice*. Cambridge, Mass.: Harvard University Press.
Regan, Tom, ed. 1980. *Matters of Life and Death*. New York: Random House.
Reiman, Jeffrey. 1985. "Justice, Civilization, and the Death Penalty." *Philosophy and Public Affairs* 14: 115–48.
Rubenstein, Richard. 1978. *The Cunning of History*. New York: Harper & Row.
Sarat, Austin, ed. 1999. *The Killing State*. New York: Oxford University Press.
Sellin, Thorsten. 1959. *The Death Penalty*. Philadelphia, Penn.: The American Law Institute.
———. 1967. *Capital Punishment*. New York: Harper & Row.
Sorrell, Tom. 1987. *Moral Theory and Capital Punishment*. Oxford: Blackwell.
Steffens, Lloyd. *Executing Justice*. 1998. Cleveland, Ohio: Pilgrim Press.
Stern, Lawrence. 1970. "Deserved Punishment, Deserved Harm, Deserved Blame." *Philosophy* 45: 317–27.
Supreme Court of South Africa. 1995. *State v. Makwanyane*.
van den Haag, Ernest. 1975. *Punishing Criminals: Concerning A Very Old and Painful Question*. New York: Basic Books.
———. 1978a. "In Defense of the Death Penalty: A legal-Practical-Moral Analysis." *Criminal Law Bulletin* 14: 51–68.
———. 1978b. "The Collapse of the Case Against Capital Punishment." *National Review*, March 31.
———. 1985a. "Refuting Reiman and Nathanson." *Philosophy and Public Affairs* 14: 165–76.
———. 1985b. "The Death Penalty Once More." *U.C. Davis Law Review* 18: 957–72.
von Hirsch, Andrew. 1976. *Doing Justice*. New York: Hill & Wang.
———. 1985. *Past or Future Crimes: Deservedness and Dangerousness in the Sentencing of Criminals*. New Brunswick, N.J.: Rutgers University Press.
Weisberg, Robert. 1984. "Deregulating Death." In *The 1983 Supreme Court Review*, edited by Philip Kurland. Chicago: University of Chicago Press.
Wilson, James Q. 1977. *Thinking About Crime*. New York: Vintage Books; Rev. ed., 1983. New York: Basic Books.
Zeisel, Hans. 1977. "The Deterrent Effect of the Death Penalty: Facts v. Faith." In *The 1976 Supreme Court Review*, edited by Philip Kurland. Chicago: University of Chicago Press.
Zimring, F. and G. Hawkins. 1973. *Deterrence*. Chicago: University of Chicago Press.
———. 1986. *Capital Punishment and the American Agenda*. Cambridge: Cambridge University Press.

Index